40 DAYS OF Refreshment

Quiet Times for Hectic Hearts

BRAD WHITT

FOREWORD BY MAC BRUNSON

Published by Innovo Publishing, LLC
www.innovopublishing.com
1-888-546-2111

Publishing quality books, eBooks, audiobooks, music, screenplays & courses for the Christian & wholesome markets since 2008.

40 Days of Refreshment
Quiet Times for Hectic Hearts

Copyright © 2023 by Brad Whitt
All rights reserved.

No part of this publication may be reproduced, stored in a retrieval system, or transmitted in any form or by any means electronic, mechanical, photocopying, recording, or otherwise, without the prior written permission of the Author.

Unless otherwise noted, all scripture is taken from the New King James Version®. Copyright © 1982 by Thomas Nelson. Used by permission. All rights reserved.

ISBN: 978-1-61314-923-2

Cover Design & Interior Layout: Innovo Publishing, LLC

Printed in the United States of America
U.S. Printing History
First Edition: 2015
Second Edition: 2023

Has God called you to create a Christ-centered or wholesome book, eBook, audiobook, music album, screenplay, or online course? Visit Innovo's educational center (cpportal.com) to learn how to accomplish your calling with excellence.

I am deeply grateful for the steadfast helpmate the Lord gave me in my sweet wife, Kim. She has enhanced and enabled my ministry for over 20 years. I joyfully dedicate this book to her and our children: Laura Kate, Jack, Benjamin, and Jonathan.

I also thank the Lord for the influence of my father in the ministry, Dr. James Merritt, who taught me to love and preach the Bible, and for the many deacons and leaders I have been privileged to serve alongside these many years.

Contents

Foreword 9

1: The Savior's First Lesson on Suffering 11
2: When God Speaks through Silence 14
3: The Sacrifice of Self 16
4: How to Be Holy 18
5: Refreshing Fire 20
6: Spiritual Anger 22
7: The Savior's Glorious Love 24
8: Empty Things 26
9: Mountaintop Moments and Valley Victories 29
10: An Unexpected Arrow 31
11: If It's True It Isn't New 34
12: The Fellowship of the Wilderness 37
13: Our Earliest Aim 40
14: Why Is Love the Greatest? 43
15: Sin's First Sign 45
16: God's Magnificent Mercy 47
17: The Christian's Responsibility of Joy 50
18: Fit for Glory 53
19: When We Need His Armor the Most 56
20: Why God Hides His Face 59
21: The Lord's Use of Adversity 61
22: The Place of Penalty's Pardon 63
23: Alone with Jesus 65

24: The Light of the Lord's Life 68
25: My Father's Hidden Hand 70
26: The Curse of Indifference 72
27: The Goodness of God's Spirit 75
28: The Strength of the Savior's Sacrifice 77
29: Temptation's Location 79
30: The Gift of a Thorn 81
31: Sacrifice at Sunset 83
32: The Light of Life 85
33: The Shield of Sacrifice 87
34: Angelic Education 89
35: The Spirit's Chiseling of Our Stony Souls 92
36: Asking in the Name of Jesus 94
37: Life in a Look 96
38: Walking with God 98
39: The Place of Worship 100
40: Thirsty for God 103

Honoring the Lord and Encouraging the Saints................105

41: Waiting for Hope 106
42: The Might of Meekness 108
43: The Law of Liberty 110
44: Hindsight Is Heavenly 112
45: The Power in Being Poor 114
46: Consecrating Common Things 116
47: The Power of Personal Ministry 118
48: The Rest Jesus Gives 120

Foreword

Can you think of all the things that have happened in *40 Days*?

- Moses lived forty years in Egypt, forty years in the desert, and forty more years leading Israel.
- Moses also spent forty days up on Mount Sinai meeting with God to get the law for the people.
- The Hebrews wandered for forty years in the wilderness, until an entire generation died.
- The prophet Jonah walked through the streets of Nineveh with just one message: "Yet forty days and Nineveh will be overthrown" (Jonah 3:4).
- For Noah and his family, it rained for forty days and forty nights on the earth.
- Ezekiel, that strange prophet, slept on his side for forty days and nights as a sign to the nation.
- Elijah went forty days without food or water.
- Jesus, in the wilderness of temptation, went forty days without food or water.
- After Jesus wept over the city, He predicted the fall of Jerusalem. It was nearly forty years after His crucifixion that the Romans burned the city.
- Jesus spent forty days appearing to His disciples after the resurrection before He ascended back to Heaven.

The number forty is fascinating as well as an important number with great significance and meaning. It is a symbol of a period of time of trials, tests, and transitions.

Every one of us goes through those periods of tests, trials, and transitions and the question is how do you prepare for them? Better yet, how do you make it through them? The best way to meet the trials and tests and transitions of life is to be prepared by being in the Word of God daily.

Foreword

Dr. Brad Whitt has prepared 40 significant daily devotionals that will not just get you through these days of transition but will grow you through the trials and tests that come your way. Every devotional is a demonstration of the power of God's Word to deepen your life and develop a helpful spiritual principle. By the end of forty days, you will also have developed a new spiritual habit, a daily devotional. This devotional, once a day for forty days, will be one of the most invaluable, life altering disciplines you could ever engage in. Don't wait until you find yourself in a transition, a trial, or a test. Begin today.

—Dr. Mac Brunson, Senior Pastor, Valleydale Church, Birmingham, AL

1

The Savior's First Lesson on Suffering

And He began to teach them that the Son of Man must suffer many things, and be rejected by the elders and chief priests and scribes, and be killed, and after three days rise again. Mark 8:31

Mark tells us that at this time Jesus "began to teach them that the Son of Man must suffer many things." This was certainly a new lesson for mankind to learn. Before this, man had been taught that a "Son of Man" should never suffer – that those who were elevated should be exempt from suffering and pain. This was a thought that was deeply rooted in the hearts of Jews and Gentiles. The Gentile bowed down before overwhelming strength—such strength would never bow down to another. The Jew honored those men who were favored with fortune's smile. These were sons of the morning, thought to be the nearest and dearest to God.

Christianity, however, began to paint a completely opposite and novel idea on the canvas of man's conscience. Christianity taught that the true test of a man's height was his capacity, not his inability, to feel. "The Son of Man *must* suffer many things…" Suffering wasn't a "might" or a "maybe"; it was an absolute certainty. Suffering is seen in the fact that He *is* the Son of Man – that He is on the mountain's height. If He were not so elevated, He would have been protected. The very position of His person placed Him in the center of sin's crucible. Don't forget that this was the very source of Jesus' time of temptation in the wilderness. The Devil came and said, "If you really are the Son of Man, then you ought to enjoy yourself. You should never have want for bread. You should never experience the fear of falling. You should never worry over the world's kingdom or lack their glory. You should live decadently, walk daringly, and rule despotically." Christ turned all of this on its head. He taught that because He is the Son of Man, He was certain to suffer—to personally experience the world's hunger for bread, fear of falling or the burden of being bound by the tyrants of the world. Even though He stands at the top, He serves as a picture of the principle for those who are climbing after Him.

There is indeed a suffering that only the good can know. There is a fire that is stoked for the man of God, a lion's den that is reserved for the holy. Not every eye can shed tears over Jerusalem—that is a supernatural and spiritual gift from God alone. The rough crowd around Christ's cross said, "Let God rescue Him if He delights in Him!" If He is so good, then why does He suffer so? The truth is that if He had *not* been so good, He wouldn't have suffered as much. It was His purity that brought His pain; His tenderness that caused His tears; His selflessness that brought His sorrow; His righteousness that caused His restlessness; His kindness that cost Him His kin; His crown that caused His cross. He didn't even have a place to lay His head—because He was the Son of Man.

Learn the lesson that Christ began to teach, that His pain can cure all other pain. There is no remedy in the world like the one whereby His sorrow overcomes all. There is nothing other than His unselfish grief that can remove my selfish care. Joy doesn't have the ability; concern would corrupt it in a matter of moments. Beauty doesn't have the desire; the dust of this life would dim it in a day. Fame doesn't have the strength; the worn heart would surely wither overnight. Wealth doesn't have the wherewithal; the power of personal toil would rip it from my soul. However, if there were a way that I could receive Heaven's remedy, then I would be healed. *He* can give it.

What a tremendous thought! To know that when He gives a new care, the old one dies. When He shares His weight, the old one is lifted. When He gives His cross, I am crowned. Listen closely to the wails of the weary, and yours will become silent. Lift the load of the poor, and yours will be lightened. Carry the weight of the weak, and yours will be removed. Listen to the sighs of the sick, and yours will suddenly cease. Share in the task of those who toil, and yours will be tearless. Touch the hand of the leper, and yours will be healed. Help the feet of the lame, and yours will rise up and run. Catch those who fall into temptation and be caught yourself. May the Son of Man's pain be a panacea for every pain in your life.

Thoughts

2

When God Speaks through Silence

When the voice had ceased, Jesus was found alone. But they kept quiet, and told no one in those days any of the things they had seen. Luke 9:36

Sometimes God speaks through silence. There are times when the Lord's voice dies upon the mountain, and the mountain shares no testimony. We cry out to Heaven but hear no answer. We question the Lord but receive no reply. Yet it is in the silence that a revelation comes in the form of a man. I descend from the summit of divine speculation to the valley of human sympathy. I see my brother because God has chosen to hide Himself. Oh, what a divine descent it is!

From the mountain's height, everything on Earth seems so small. Its crosses shrink in the infinite light of eternity, and I am prone to be unsympathetic to the pain of the human heart. The worn and weary's cries are lost amidst the songs and shouts of the redeemed. That's why many times my Heavenly Father comes to me in silence's chariot. He hides Himself from my sight. He shuts the door to the sacred sanctuary. He pulls a cloud over His great glory. He makes me looks down, not up. He draws my attention from the crown to the cross. He causes me to focus not on Heaven's opening but Earth's imprisoned. He points me to the solitary Savior—Jesus alone. He shows me Jesus without His pomp, power, or kingdom. He reveals the weakened form of Christ sinking under the weight of humanity's sinful woe. God's silence reveals man.

If you constantly beat in vain against eternity's problems, turn aside and be set free. Sometimes God speaks through silence. He says to stop gazing up to Heaven. He says that you're not ready for life on the mount. He calls you to come back to the plain—from the search for the divine to sympathy for mankind. His silence shrouds your face like Moses' and teaches you to be meek by the loss of vision. Listen to His silence and learn from it. Go down and kneel next to Jesus under darkened heavens; wait and watch with Him in His humiliating hour. Walk with Him down among mankind to sense and share their agony. You will miss nothing in the divine silence if you will only find Jesus alone.

Thoughts

3

The Sacrifice of Self

He shall see the travail of His soul, and be satisfied. By His knowledge My righteous Servant shall justify many, For He shall bear their iniquities. Isaiah 53:11

Never before had God seen a soul's travail. Sure, He had received countless offerings of the body as, down through the ages, sacrificial fires had blazed, torturing their involuntary victims. But never before had there been the surrender of the human will, the travail of the human soul. Thus, the heart of the Heavenly Father was never satisfied until there came One who was willing to delight in doing His will. But when Jesus came, all other sacrifices ceased. He came giving nothing but Himself—His very soul. From Bethlehem's manger, He poured out His soul unto death. From daybreak to midday, He climbed the heights of Calvary. One by one He gave up the stages of His being. He surrendered His childhood in subjection, turned over His youth to toil, and delivered His manhood by walking down the Dolorosa. This was the travail of His soul.

Don't you know it is you that the Father desires most? He doesn't want your pains or possessions, your gifts or griefs, your trinkets or tortures. He wants you. He desires nothing more from you than your will to give all of yourself. Has He come and commanded that you give your beloved Isaac? If so, it is not really Isaac He wants. His desire is for you, and it is a desire that never ceases. Do you doubt this is true? Then get up early in the morning and march to Moriah. Carry in your arms that which you love and offer it on the sacrifice of your will. Then you will hear a small voice behind you saying, "Don't hurt the boy or do anything to him; for now I know…"

Give Him your will, and He will ask nothing more. Give Him your heart, and He will give back all of your gifts with interest—the interest of selfless joy. Your Isaac will be returned to you when you have reached the sacrificial summit of Moriah. Earth will be poured back into your life when you have first sought His kingdom and righteousness. You will no longer be asked to sacrifice when you have surrendered your spirit, for the spirit that has been first broken by love is surely the soul's travail.

Thoughts

_____
_____
_____
_____
_____
_____
_____
_____
_____

4

How to Be Holy

Let us know, Let us pursue the knowledge of the LORD. His going forth is established as the morning; He will come to us like the rain, Like the latter and former rain to the earth. Hosea 6:3

To "know the Lord" is indeed an audacious aim for a finite soul. Yet I find that my soul is satisfied with nothing less. Night and day, I beat at the walls of my prison. I struggle with the mystery that surrounds my being. I long for the only Light that can make sense of the darkness. I would surely be content just to touch the hem of the Master's garment as He passes by. However, to "know Him," to *really* "know Him," is no doubt the greatest gift of life everlasting.

Surprisingly I discover that it is not through searching for God that I find Him. It is only through following Him that He is ultimately known. This knowledge is not found at the beginning of life, but rather at the end of life. It doesn't come in the spring but the summer. It is seen in the bloom, not the bud. It isn't the embryo of my experience but the fruit of a faithful walk with Him.

If I were to have some miraculous, magnificent vision of God, would this make me like Him? No. The prophet says that it is only by following after Him that I can truly know Him. Practice is the alphabet of heavenly knowledge. Do you desire to know His doctrine? Then you must do what He says. Would you want to see God? Then you must be pure in heart. Do you want to see Him as He truly is? Then you must first be like Him.

God is love. Of course, He has other attributes, but love is His chief characteristic. It is what He is, and only love can look upon love. Can you hear music with your eyes or see colors with your ears? No, and it's with no other organ than the heart that you can look upon love. It is the heart that is the sense that can see God, and it is the heart that is the life of love. So if you will walk with Him daily, you will learn to know Him, and by knowing Him more you will come to love what He loves. When you have followed Him into the Garden of Gethsemane, you will know as you are known.

Thoughts

5

Refreshing Fire

While I was musing, the fire burned... Psalm 39:3

Have you ever stopped to consider the fact that if you would spend more time musing, or meditating, the fire of your soul would burn brighter and hotter? You see, it is because we spend so little time in meditation and reflection that we often have so little exhilaration and enthusiasm in our walk with the Lord. Why, then, don't you withdraw from the world more often to spend time with the Lord? If you do, you would soon discover that you would be better equipped to face the world because you would be, in fact, less worldly.

One of the most detrimental and devastating results of our nonstop, fast-paced, hectic and high-tech world is that we no longer make time to get alone with God. We don't withdraw to spend time with Him. We don't take the opportunity to reflect on His Word, will, and working in our lives. That's why we are so cold and calloused, and lack greatness even as other men consider greatness. If there were more of the fire of Heaven in our hearts, we would have more power here on earth.

Is there no secret place where you can go to warm yourself? Is there no Holy of Holies where you can get a glimpse of the flame of God to strengthen your soul? Don't forget, everything that has been great and stirred the world hasn't come from without, but from within. Doesn't the Bible even say that as Jesus "prayed, the fashion of his countenance was altered, and his raiment *was* white *and* glistering"? Yes, it was from His prayer that the power for His transfigured glory came. It was, in essence, the glow from His heart that shone on His face. It was when the Lord Jesus was musing that the fire burned!

Do you desire to see your life glorified, beautified, and transfigured in the eyes of men? Then get up to the top of the mountain. Get alone with God in the secret place where the fires of His love burn bright. Climb to the crest of contemplation, where you can catch the fresh breezes of Heaven, where the winds of the Spirit can fan the flame of your soul. Then your life will radiate gloriously to those down on the plain—and even more so because you will be unconscious of the glory of its shining. Your prayers will illuminate your face like Moses' when he didn't know that it shone so. Your words will burn, kindling the hearts of others like those who walked with the Lord to Emmaus. Your path will be lit by the Lord's lamp as written by the Psalmist. It is when you have prayed in solitude as Elijah that you will catch a ride in a chariot of fire.

Thoughts

_____

_____

_____

_____

_____

_____

_____

6

Spiritual Anger

Then the Spirit of God came upon Saul when he heard this news, and his anger was greatly aroused. 1 Samuel 11:6

This seems to be a rather strange response of the Spirit. In fact, I would have expected any other response than this. I have always understood that the presence of the Spirit means love. Yet here I am told that its purpose was to create anger in King Saul. Does that mean that there is a love that is compatible with anger? I believe that the answer is "yes."

In the book of Revelation, I read about "the wrath of the Lamb." Isn't that an odd statement? Does that mean that the Lamb lost the presence of the Spirit and suddenly burst into anger? Absolutely not. In fact, I believe that it is the Spirit's presence that gives Him His wrath.

There is an anger that comes from the spirit of man, and there is an anger that comes from the Spirit of God. The anger of man resents the *hurt*; but the anger of the Spirit resents the *wrong*. The anger of man reacts because his pride has been wounded, but the anger of the Spirit responds because His heart has been wounded. Man's anger rages that he has been injured, but the Spirit's anger grieves that God has been injured. Man's anger cries for revenge, but the Spirit's anger cries out for atonement.

The Spirit of Christ has come to consecrate the whole of my human nature—including my anger. He hasn't come to destroy my personality, but rather redeem it from destruction. There have been times in my life when I shouldn't have been angry, but I was. There have also been times in my life when I should have been angry, but I wasn't. I have been angry because the gourd withered, but I wasn't angry over what caused it to wither. I am eager to avenge the result of some personal offense, but I'm not so eager to deal with the root of the offense.

One reason why I so desperately need the Spirit's personal presence is so He can create in me a profound, divine horror over that which blights the gourd. I need to be inspired with a love that hates hate, despises scorn, and rages against injustice. I need Him to stir up within my spirit a great groaning in which my tears do not come from weakness but are born of a holy passion against hatred, contentions, jealousies, outbursts of wrath, selfish ambitions, dissensions, and heresies. I need Him to fan in my heart a fiery zeal that burns with a holy hatred over those things that destroy life's temple.

So often the passions of my heart are owned by my own selfishness and sin. May they be transformed into the Lord's righteousness and be used for His service. For when His fire baptizes my heart, I will know what it truly means to "be angry, and sin not."

Thoughts

7

The Savior's Glorious Love

And the Word became flesh and dwelt among us, and we beheld His glory, the glory as of the only begotten of the Father, full of grace and truth. John 1:14

The fullness of grace and truth in the person of Jesus was indeed glorious. It was the coming together of two things that are so often opposites in the hearts of men. Some souls easily display grace. There is a natural forgiveness that they give to others, but they have a low view of the divine truth that has been violated. Then there are those who have a clear understanding of the majesty of divine truth and an overwhelming sense of repulsion towards the sin that rebels against it, but often these are unable to forgive the trespasser. There is more truth than grace. John tells us that in the person of Jesus, however, we find something altogether unexpected. We find in Him the perfect blending of two opposites. In Christ, we see the fullness of grace perfectly united with absolute truth.

There is forgiveness that has no value because it has no sense of wrong, and there is a sense of wrong that repels because there is no ability to forgive. In Christ, there is fullness of forgiveness combined with total truth. The glorious thing about the love of Jesus is that it comes from light, not darkness. He forgives sinners because He bore in His body their sin. There was never a time when His forgiveness was fuller than when He bore His fullest witness to the terrible truth of the sin of man.

When did Jesus cry out, "Father, forgive them, for they know not what they do," was it at the time when He first began to see our sin as a simple slip-up or just a small violation of God's law? No, it was when the violated law was stabbing His heart and the reproach of our sin was breaking His body. His love comes from His pity, and His pity was born of His purity. He knew that we had lost what He calls our soul. He knew that we were blind in a world of beauty, deaf in a world of song, cold in a warm world and dead in a world pulsing with life. That's why He looked up to the veiled face of the Father and cried, "I'm covered in their darkness—give them light. I'm bruised by their sorrow—give to them joy. I'm shivering in their coldness—give them warmth. I'm dying their death—give them eternal life."

Calvary was the hour of Christ's greatest glory. It was there, like the subtle shades of a rainbow, that colors that had never before been combined were joined—justice and forgiveness, righteousness and peace, penalty and pardon, the verdict of death and the pronouncement of life. Heaven and Earth met, judgment and mercy embraced, and grace and truth stood shoulder to shoulder. The moment of sin's greatest condemnation was the time of the world's fullest redemption. This is the glory of the Savior's love.

Thoughts

_____

_____

_____

_____

_____

8

Empty Things

And do not turn aside; for then you would go after empty things which cannot profit or deliver, for they are nothing. 1 Samuel 12:21

What a strange, and even anticlimactic, statement! Samuel says to the people that they must not turn aside from God. That certainly makes sense, but his reason is rather startling. He says that if they deviate from following the Lord, they will end up going "after empty things." Okay, I get it. They would fall for the frivolous, but is that the worst thing that could happen? Is it really all that bad that those who detour from following after God would go after those things that are "nothing"?

Why does Samuel have such a great fear of emptiness? Certainly it is always a terrible thing to stop following after God. But if the worst thing that a man could do is give himself to shallow, frivolous, and empty-headed pursuits, is that really so terrible? Wouldn't it be better to go after the simple, harmless, innocent things of this world—things that would be considered "silly"—rather than give yourself to those things that are indeed "sinful"? Samuel says, "No."

Who is the furthest away from God? Which one would take longer to come back to Him? Is it the one who was lured by lust? The one who slipped into open sin? The one who hurt his own heart with acts of debauchery? No, all of these have come quickly to Christ. Mary Magdalene's passion was transformed for Jesus. Saul's fiery hatred of Christ was turned into a fiery love for Him. Peter's guilt was changed to glory. Each of these had no doubt been far from the Lord. It appears far more difficult for those who have simply become caught up with the common cares of this world to come to Christ than those who were deep in sin. Simon the Pharisee is "further away" than Mary Magdalene because he's "empty."

What is the opposite of a calm sea? Is it a sea stirred by a great storm? No, because in a minute it can go from stormy to settled, from raging to peaceful, from windy to complete and utter calm. No, the opposite of a calm sea isn't a stormy sea. It is a stale, stagnant pool. Why? Because it is missing the very thing found in both the stormy and the settled sea. It is missing life.

There is nothing so detrimental to fellowship with God as the worship of trifling things because such worship is idolatry without any sense of sin. Trifles don't trouble the human heart, and like Bethesda, where there is no troubling of the pool, there can never be any healing.

May the Lord deliver me from lifting up my heart to vain, empty, trifling things. There is a pride that lifts itself only to bring about its own fall. It's when I set my sights on those things that are surely impossible that I see my own presumption. However, when I take aim at those things that are beneath me, then I fail to realize my great need. I am lulled into a false sense of achievement by the simplicity of my aim.

If I were to set out to scale the Tower of Babel, my failure would immediately be evident and would likely cause me to see my failure and need of forgiveness. But when I build my house on the sand, and it stands, I see no sin and therefore realize no need for God. So when Jesus comes walking on the stormy seas, I don't even see that I'm sinking and that I must reach up and cry out to Him.

Great sinners such as Zacchaeus and Mary have come—but not me. Why? Because there are times that my amazing selfishness is held in such a small vessel. "My sin isn't as great as Zacchaeus'. It isn't as notorious as Mary's. Surely it is a small thing that I haven't helped my neighbor or shared a kind word." I have hidden my treasure in a trifle, and it is the trifling thing that now hides Him from me.

Oh, that He would rend the veil and show me the tragedy of the trifle! How I pray to see the great poison that is contained in such a tiny box. May Christ break the box and trample on the trifling things of my life. May He teach me to know just how much I desperately need Him. May I then follow only after Him and not be turned aside by "empty things."

Thoughts

_____

_____

_____

_____

_____

_____

_____

_____

_____

9

Mountaintop Moments and Valley Victories

Then Peter answered and said to Jesus, "Rabbi, it is good for us to be here; and let us make three tabernacles: one for You, one for Moses, and one for Elijah." Mark 9:5

Peter had just experienced the most wonderful, powerful event in his life. He had been caught up in the glory, taken to the summit of the mount with his master, the Lord Jesus. The sights of his surroundings and the constant murmur of men had overshadowed his world with a sense of glory that he had never known before. For a moment, for a brief moment, he had lost himself and wanted nothing more than to forget everything and everybody that he had ever known and stay on that mountaintop forever. The temporal things of the world had become his enemy, and he no longer wanted anything to do with them. He wanted to rise above them in rapture, stand on the summit in victory, and set up an eternal tabernacle on that mountain top.

How many times have I wished for the same? How many sweet times of fellowship with my Lord have I longed to have last forever? When I gathered at His table and took the cup and the bread in my hand in remembrance of Him, or during the nights that I spent at the altar in prayer, how often did I wish to set up a tabernacle in that place?

But too soon I heard the stirring of people, the hushed voices of those around me, the doors open and cars start up as life began to move again. I have often mourned over having to leave that special place too soon. "Why do I have to go back? Why can't I just stay here? This is a good thing. This is a special place. I don't want to leave! Why must I always leave the quiet place to return to the roar of the battle? Why won't my Lord allow me to do what Peter asked and make for Him a tabernacle here?"

The answer I have received is the one given to Peter—"Get up and go! This is not your rest." You see, men were not made for the mountain. We were made for the valley. The place that is best suited for the soul of man is not the mountain of glory but the valley of ministry. At the foot of the mountain is a demoniac who needs to be delivered. His cries come up the cliffs from the valley of his humiliation. Am I too good to enter into his tent of suffering? Am I above being a help to those bound up by sin?

So, then, the cloud that veils His heavenly vision is really my glory. It is drawn for my good. The storm that sends me back down the mountain is indeed my tabernacle of rest. It calls to me from the valley, from those who are sick and sorrowful and sinful and says, "Build your tabernacle here!"

Thoughts

_____

_____

_____

_____

_____

_____

10

An Unexpected Arrow

Now a certain man drew a bow at random, and struck the king of Israel between the joints of his armor... 2 Chronicles 18:33

It's a rather strange story that suggests a unique, and often overlooked, truth. Ahab, though he was the king of Israel, was seen as the enemy of God by the faithful and the enemy of man by everybody else. In fact, they had made elaborate plans to remove him from his position, but every plan they'd tried had failed. They had sent squads and entire armies to kill him, but nothing succeeded. They had even aimed all of their arrows at him, but every arrow missed its royal target. Then something very strange and completely unexpected happened. An unnamed soldier was wasting time, perhaps trying some trick shots with his bow and arrow for the amusement of his friends or himself. Suddenly the trick shot became a tragic shot when the arrow meant for another target found its way to the enemy of God and he fell dead. The killing of the king came from a hand that wasn't looking to take a life and from an arrow that wasn't meant for him.

This isn't as unusual an occurrence as we might at first think. How many times, with little or no effort, do we get something that we have worked and struggled for so long in vain? We plan and work and try and suddenly out of nowhere we find that for which we labored so long lying on our doorstep. We spend hours or days trying to remember a name, and suddenly it jumps into our mind when we were actually thinking about something else. You work long and hard, but when you finally give up your effort, that which you worked for so long and hard comes to pass. Growing up I often heard that "a watched pot never boils." It seems that there is truth to this statement. I've come to believe that so many times it is the thing we are the most anxious to accomplish that never happens. In fact, personal observation says that all of our effort may even serve to divert our arrows to another target.

When God promised Abraham that He would create from him a great and mighty kingdom, the Lord added, "all the peoples of the earth will be blessed through you." He had tried his entire life to make a name for himself, and suddenly he was going to get the former by shooting at the latter. Even though it stands in opposition to everything we are told today, I have never known a man to attain personal success by making personal success his one and only aim. So many times the prize is hit by aiming at something entirely different. David sang to sheep in the woods but was heard by kings. Mary broke the box of precious perfume to anoint the head of Jesus but ended up filling the entire house with its fragrance. The arrow that hits the target of the greatest everlasting honor is often the one that was aimed at the simplest need of the day.

Be very careful of the direction in which you aim your life. How many books have we seen entitled, "How To Achieve Success," or "How To Win"? I would suggest that such goals not be the aim of your life. True success often comes from aiming at other things.

The motto of the age tells us that "work brings wealth." I agree that we ought to work, but I would add that we must work at things that the world considers to be a waste of time. I would tell you to work at love—for the benefit of those around you. The world tells us to make friends to open doors. No doubt our relationships can, and often will, open up doors that would have been closed to us otherwise. However, I would caution you to make friends not for what they can do for you, but simply because true friends add value and beauty to your life. The world says that those things you do now, the hard work and long hours you invest now, will help you later on in life. There's no doubt that this is often proven to be true. But I would suggest you aim for the grave, not just the gold.

Your arrow may hit earthly fruit and drop it into your lap, but let it do so by accident. Don't aim for the fruit. Aim for the flower or the leaf. If you will seek first His kingdom and His righteousness, then the blessings of the king will be yours also. If you'll seek purity, you will find peace. If you'll seek friendship, you will find fortune. If you'll seek goodness, you will find glory. If you'll seek sobriety, you will find strength. If you'll see wisdom, you will find wealth. If you'll seek reflection, you will find reputation. If you'll seek benevolence, you will find blessing. If you'll seek Christ first, you will find His cup and with it, great joy. When you shoot your arrow at an unselfish goal, you will find that it will bring an unexpected gain to your life.

Thoughts

11

If It's True It Isn't New

But we have renounced the hidden things of shame, not walking in craftiness nor handling the word of God deceitfully, but by manifestation of the truth commending ourselves to every man's conscience in the sight of God. 2 Corinthians 4:2

I once heard my pastor Adrian Rogers say, "If it's true, it isn't new." Had the Apostle Paul heard him, he would have given a loud and hearty "Amen!" I say this because I believe it is the essence of Paul's point in this statement to the church at Corinth. I understand Paul to teach that there shouldn't be anything purely original in a revelation. When he writes about "commending ourselves to every man's conscience," I believe he's talking about commending truth to the "consciousness" of man. Paul's point is that divine truth, like any other truth, must first speak to man's experience. It must appeal to something that the hearer already knows to be true. In other words it, is "a faithful saying worthy of all acceptation."

To be sure, this is not the normal way of thinking. Most people believe divine revelation must be something that is completely and totally new. They believe that if God wants to speak or reveal something to man that He will say something that man has never heard before. This is certainly the way most people view "getting a fresh word from God." They hear a sermon and God speaks to them, and they say something like, "That was a fresh word from God. I had never seen that before." What do they mean? Do they mean that it was a completely new and novel thought? I don't think so. I believe what they mean to say is that they recognized something that wasn't expected. It was a fresh thought that was discovered once the Holy Spirit pulled the veil aside. It didn't suddenly appear out of nowhere. It had been there all along, covered by the veil. Finding it, in the most literal of sense, was truly a discovery. It was the removal of something that had covered and concealed it from view. When it was seen, it was immediately recognized as something that had belonged to them all along, something that they never should have been without. It's not something strange, but oddly familiar. The freshness of the revelation comes from the fact that while it wasn't consciously known, it had been there all along.

Paul says that this is true with regard to the revelation of God's truth. Yes, it is divine in its nature, but it presents itself to the consciousness of man and appeals to his personal experience. In fact, this is the simplest meaning of the word "revelation." It speaks of pulling aside the veil to see something that had always been there. It's not talking about creating something absolutely new, but rather uncovering something old. It has been wrapped up, covered, concealed, lying just within reach all throughout our lives without our knowing that it was there.

What God's revelation—His light—reveals to me is actually myself. He has hung a mirror in my room that all during the night I thought was simply a dark, blank spot on the wall. However, when the sun began to rise and I saw by His light the reflection of my heart in His mirror, it was then that I really realized I was a man.

Don't ever forget that God has distinct voices for different souls—He speaks to the conscience of every man. And even though His light "lights every man that comes into the world," it doesn't have the same beam for every soul. God shines into separate rooms, each one furnished differently, of man's heart. Do I have the right to require that my brother's room be furnished the same way as mine? Elijah's table was spread in the desert and what he needed was a human voice, so God sent him a friend. Peter's food came to him in dreams—let down on a sheet from Heaven. What he needed was to be woken by reality, so God sent him into a stormy sea. John expected to immediately be seated at Jesus' right hand. What he needed was to learn how to patiently wait, so God sent him on a long journey that ended on the rocky outcroppings of Patmos. Paul had the burden of too much light and was prone to be unappreciative of a brother's difficulty. What he needed was the experience of human weakness, so God sent him a thorn in the flesh. Matthew had too many thorns. Everywhere he went he faced hardship, contempt, hatred, and scorn. He didn't need God to give another thorn, but a flower. So he received a revelation of the Lord's presence in a feast.

I, for one, am thankful to God that not only does He knock on every heart's door, but that He always varies His knocking. He called quietly to Martha. He met Mary in a social setting. He cried with a loud voice to Lazarus. Today He supplies my life not where it is the strongest, but where it is the weakest. He knows me better than I know myself, and He loves me enough that He reaches into my conscience through my consciousness of need.

Thoughts

_____

_____

_____

_____

_____

_____

_____

12

The Fellowship of the Wilderness

*And the LORD said to Aaron, "Go into the wilderness to meet Moses."
So he went and met him on the mountain of God… Exodus 4:27*

God told Aaron to go out into the wilderness and meet Moses. That seems very strange to me because the wilderness wasn't normally a place that a person would go for social interaction. It was a lonely, isolated place. It was the place where people who were shunned and ostracized would be driven from the presence of others—deprived of the means of being useful to themselves or anybody else.

Now, when God calls one to go to the great cities, the hubs of human interaction, that makes sense to us. It seems logical that a person can be of most use to God in the midst of multitudes of people. But when God calls a person out into the wilderness—when He puts him in a hospital bed or places on his shoulders a heavy burden—something says deep within our souls, "That's not the way it's supposed to be. That doesn't make any sense. What purpose could God possibly have in this wasteland?" We would have said the same thing if we had been there with Aaron when God called him to the wilderness. "Go into the wilderness…"

Now, I don't know how the call came, but most likely it would have come during a time of either mental exhaustion or physical abandonment, much like what happened in the life of Elijah after the showdown on Mount Carmel. If that is the case, then there is something in me that lurches forward in pity for the poor man. My flesh would want to say that his life is over, but in reality his life was just beginning, and it was beginning through this apparent end. You see, when he went out from his world into His wilderness he walked right into the arms of his destiny.

"Go into the wilderness to meet Moses." This was God's plan, written in Heaven and revealed to Aaron, and it seems simple enough. He had met Moses hundreds, if not thousands, of times. Moses was his brother. They had grown up together, lived together, spent countless hours together. So the question going through his mind as he walked out into the wilderness must have been, "How in the world can meeting Moses change my destiny?" You probably had the same thought. But when we ask that question, allow it to cross our mind unchallenged, we forget one thing. A person's destiny many times turns on the beginning of a new set of circumstances. Something may happen to us a thousand times, and the thousand and first time may bring a crisis that brings a change.

No doubt Saul of Tarsus had seen a thousand suns, but the sun on the Damascus road was one too many for him. Aaron had met Moses many times, but this meeting in the wilderness was to reveal each of them in a new light. Their common connection there in the wilderness was meant to knit their hearts together in a way that had never happened before.

My caution to you would be to not reject those wilderness moments. Don't reject those times when your spirit is broken. Think about that alabaster box broken for Jesus. If it had realized the fact that it had been broken, it might well have agreed with Judas: "Why waste it here and now and for this purpose?" But the answer was found as that fragrance filled the entire house. Its triumph was found in its tragedy.

It's the same way in our lives. We are never truly useful—or usable—to Him until we have first had that wilderness experience because it is out there in the wilderness that we are connected with our kind.

I've often thought about two of the initial incidents in the life of Jesus—the wilderness and the wedding at Cana—and wondered which one was the loneliest for Him? After reflection, I think it must have been Cana because this was a place that He would not be again, whereas He would spend many days and nights out in the wilderness. Cana is not a place where everybody would visit, but the wilderness is. We all have our times of triumph, but none of us rejoices in the same way over the same things. Our mountains are not normally shared, but our valleys often are. We don't use the label "happy" for the same things as everybody else, but "sad" is placed on the same things by all—death, pain, sickness, sorrow, failure, weariness.

You see, it is the cross, not the crown, that is the symbol of our connection.

Thoughts

13

Our Earliest Aim

I love them that love me; and those that seek me early shall find me.
Prov. 8:17

It is the boldest, greatest aim that any marksman could ever take—to seek God. But to tell the marksman to take his earliest aim at his greatest object is surely one of the most paradoxical statements ever uttered, as well. We certainly don't teach a beginner to take his first aim at the object that is farthest away. No. We put a large target up close, well within his reach. We operate under the principle that it is better to begin with that which is closer, easier, and then move to the more distant, difficult object.

Here, however, we are taught an opposite truth. We are not told to move from less to more, from the easiest to the hardest, from the smallest to the greatest. Our God says, "Let your earliest aim be at the greatest, highest, best—Me!" In essence, God is telling us that if we wish to be successful spiritual marksmen, we must make it our aim to hit the farthest object first. The beginning object of our imitation shouldn't be some other person, but God. Our earliest aim should be our highest.

We see this daily in the world around us. The things that most stimulate and excite us are not those of a lower, inferior form—the cheap knockoffs—but those which are the highest, greatest, best. I would much rather be bathed in sunlight than in candlelight. My children are more excited about the dawning of a new day when I throw open the blinds and they see the sun than they are when I just turn on the light.

This principle is true not only in the natural world, but also in the spiritual world. That's why I must point my children to God before anything or anybody else. I must teach them to focus on the Eternal One who is altogether lovely, not on physical beauty that is fleshly and fleeting. I must not lead them into and leave them in the outer court, but into the Holy of Holies, where He who is highest reigns supreme. I would have them move from God to man than from man to God.

I say to you, "Before anything else, aim for the heavens!" Don't take your first aim at those things that are on the ground. Don't say to yourself, "I'll start low and slow and when I grow comfortable with that. Then I will gradually begin to take higher aim." Aim your earliest arrow at He who is the highest. Seek after God early in the morning. Don't follow some mortal man's path to Heaven; follow Jesus! Don't measure your life by the world's greatest philosophers, professors, or preachers. Measure your life by Christ's! Don't even pattern your life after an angel. Pattern your life after the One who is better than the angels!

Don't think that it is best to first try to imitate the life that you can most easily reach. Reach for the One who is unreachable. To be sure, you will never reach such a lofty and holy goal, but that's the glory of it all. You will always have Him as the greatest, highest, best model. Think about it. What glory is there in reaching the ideal? Your excitement, exhilaration, and aspiration would cease. Your wings would fold and fall. That which will strengthen you for the flight is the fact that your flight will never be over.

Poets write of hills that are everlasting. Climber, that is what you need—a summit that not only can never be seen, but one that can never be reached. Christ is just such a hill of holiness. His supreme summit will be just as far after a day's worth of climbing as it was when you first set out in the morning. The glory is found in the climbing, not in the reaching of the goal. Those whose souls seek Him will find the One who is the eternal forerunner, so seek Him early!

Thoughts

___
___
___
___
___
___
___
___
___
___
___

14

Why Is Love the Greatest?

Love never fails. But whether there are prophecies, they will fail; whether there are tongues, they will cease; whether there is knowledge, it will vanish away. 1 Corinthians 13:8

Whenever we approach the beginning of a new year, many preachers, teachers, and hometown philosophers will no doubt say that it should remind us that all earthly things are perishing and passing away. I see it differently. To me the passing of the old and the beginning of the new are actually reminders of those things that are not perishing, that are not passing away. In fact, what is so wonderful about the passing years is not what they take away, but rather what they leave behind.

I believe that Paul would agree. He wasn't amazed that prophets would fail or tongues would cease or even that knowledge would vanish from sight. The thing that stirred his soul was the truth that love would never fail. Thus, his amazing lesson to all is that love is everlasting.

You see, the things that flitter and flee don't give us any assurance. Such security comes only from those things that are permanent. We feel this in our souls when we stand before the majestic mountains, not the flowing streams. Why? Because there is a greater sense of stability in the mountain than the stream.

So, then, why is love the greatest? Because it is both the oldest, and at the same time youngest, thing in all of the world. It is endless, timeless, dateless, and its unchanging nature should be on our mind and in our heart as we come to another new year. You see, the heart is one thing that the years roll over in vain. Everything else within you may tire and collapse. The speaker's voice grows weak and thin. The singer's voice becomes shrill. The businessman may lose his acumen. The politician may lose his predictive ability. The mind may become forgetful of the great riches it once discovered. But the heart—the heart—it blossoms in the dead of winter and flourishes even in the snow. It has no need of tongues because even when the voice is too weak to speak, the soul can still sing. It has no need of prophecy because when sight cannot see through the cloud, faith can still shout, "Oh grave, where is your victory?" It has no need of knowledge because when the laws of physics are forgotten, the rooms of the Father's house are still seen by love.

So don't read from today's faded leaf. You are still young at heart! Love is still as new and strong today as it was when Ruth replied, "Entreat me not to leave you, or to turn back from following after you." It was dawning that day, and it dawns still today. Love stood on Ararat when all of life was young and didn't see the flood, but the rainbow. It stood on Nebo when life was old and to this day looks out over the Promised Land. Its eyes are not dimmed, and its strength still remains. Your new day will dawn at the end of years. Heaven and Earth will pass away, but love will never fail.

Thoughts

_____
_____
_____
_____
_____

15

Sin's First Sign

And he sent them to Bethlehem and said, "Go and search carefully for the young Child, and when you have found Him, bring back word to me, that I may come and worship Him also." Matthew 2:8

Well, there you have it. Sin never shows itself to be sin in the beginning. If it did so, we would naturally be repulsed and repelled. If sin were to come to a young man or woman and say, "I'm wicked and evil. I'm going to destroy your life. Follow me," surely no one would accept its invitation.

You see, Satan's spell is broken when he shows himself, when he openly declares his desire that everybody fall down and worship him. However, that is not how he comes at first. He first comes not wearing his normal attire but appearing as an angel of light. He doesn't display himself as he truly is—the opponent and enemy of Christ—but as Christ's supporter and friend.

What makes sin so attractive? Simply that it doesn't at first appear to be sin. The appeal of vice is that it appears in the beginning to be virtue. It dresses up in another's clothes. It assumes a freedom—counterfeit freedom—that only belongs to the Master's Spirit. It calls to the young and immature to cast their cares and concerns aside as a counterfeit to those who truly cast their cares on the Lord. It promotes the possibility of self-abandonment, which is a counterfeit to the true surrender of self in the life of the Christian. It commands him to shake off the shackles of all authority and come to the freedom of such open places as a counterfeit to such true holiness that says, "I have died to the law so that I might live unto God."

Be very wary of the seeming similarities of the kingdom of Herod and the kingdom of Christ. There has never been, nor can there ever be, an alliance between the two. Their likeness lies only on the surface. The similarities are only seen on their exterior. License is not real freedom; licentiousness is not liberty; recklessness is not victory over self-concern; giving and living for yourself is not manliness. Go, search diligently for the Christ-child, and when you have found Him, you will find that Herod could never have really worshipped Him. Their dissimilarity will be seen more and more as they stand beside each other. Herod asks what seems at the beginning as a simple and trifling tribute, but it ends with you becoming his slave. Christ will accept nothing less than your heart, your life, your strength, your mind, your all, but in the end it is He and only He who can set you free. It is not Herod, but such a star of unselfish hope that will lead you to the place where "you will find the babe, wrapped in swaddling clothes and lying in a manger."

Thoughts

_____

_____

_____

_____

_____

_____

_____

16

God's Magnificent Mercy

I will not execute the fierceness of My anger; I will not again destroy Ephraim. For I am God, and not man… Hosea 11:9

It's an original, unusual, unique statement. We would have expected something completely and totally different—even from the prophet himself. He has been expressing in the clearest, starkest, strongest, loudest terms possible his sense of the divine horror of sin. He has been sharing from the lips of God the most withering, the most scathing denunciations of the evil around man. With this as a backdrop, we would expect that there would follow something like this—"I will utterly and completely destroy these wicked men. I will wipe them from the face of the Earth and from the memory of all of creation." But instead there comes this startling statement—"I will not execute the fierceness of My anger…For I am God, and not man…"

The reason why I say that this statement is so startling is because a sudden calm is as startling as a sudden storm. The wind has been rising—climbing step by step up the ladder of the Almighty's indignation—when all of a sudden it dramatically drops. It doesn't calm down. It doesn't gradually subside. It doesn't moderate over time.

It drops immediately. It goes down in a moment, in the twinkling of an eye.

My brother-in-law has spent time in India, and he says that it goes from night to day without a dawn. That's the kind of movement we find in this verse. In a second, God's frown turns into a smile. But perhaps the strangest thing that I find in this verse is the reason that is given for His leniency—"For I am God, and not man…" Startling.

One would think this would be a reason that would be given for a more drastic sentence. The normal, natural way of thinking about it would be that if the calloused conscience of your brother condemns you to death, then how much more so would an all-holy God? But Hosea says, "That's not the way it is with God." To Him the strongest is the gentlest; the purest is the most compassionate. That's exactly the way the Lord is because He is the One who most condemns sin, most feels its wickedness and most sees its evil effects.

You see, man overestimates his power of resistance. He has far less sense of sin's horror, but the eye of the Almighty sees how sin has shattered even your power of will—and so He extends pity. Who else would we run to, then? Man had no place for the leper—he sent him to live in a graveyard. At first it would be tempting to run to another human, after all, "He is a man; he is human." He knows how this frailty feels. He'll remember that we're both dust, but this is where I find my mistake. My hope is not found in the lowest, but the highest. My pardon comes from the One I thought would be the most impossible—the Sinless. I had put my hope in the compassion of a heart that is itself impure. I hoped for great things from Simon Peter for, after all, he had passed through the sea and he had experienced the wave. But when he came to Antioch, he stayed away from me; he pretended that he didn't know me. The waves of the Sea of Galilee had washed him so clean that he could no longer be a comfortable companion. But that's when Jesus came to me! He came when my friends forsook me. He came when my comrades crept away. He came when no one would even give me pig slop, when my brother denied me music and dancing. He came with the robe and the ring, through the fire and the flood, through the storm and the stress, the mist and the mire, desert and death. He came to my cloud on the mount of transfiguration. Everybody else ran when they saw my cloud—Elijah, Moses, Peter, James, and John—and I was left only seeing Jesus. That's why from this point forward, on this mountain, I will not build a tabernacle to anybody but HIM!

Thoughts

17

The Christian's Responsibility of Joy

But let all those rejoice who put their trust in You; Let them ever shout for joy, because You defend them; Let those also who love Your name Be joyful in You. Psalm 5:11

The Psalmist isn't so much sharing a promise as he is giving a command. He says to those who trust in the Lord that it is not just our responsibility to be joyful, but to make sure that everybody around us knows that we are full of the joy of the Lord, as well. In fact, the Psalmist says that it's not just our duty to "rejoice," but to "shout for joy." So, then, joyfulness is much more than mere privilege; it is our divine duty.

I believe the idea behind this command is found in the fact that to be downcast and despairing is unfitting for those of us who know and have experienced the blessings of the Lord. The Psalmist desires that there be many—multitudes—of exuberant, extravagant worshippers of our great God. That's why he's so frustrated with the very idea that the world would be considered to have a corner on joy or happiness. So he calls upon those who know God, and worship the Lord, to right that mistaken impression.

In essence, the Psalmist says, "If you really love the Lord, don't let the world think that your God is some sort of cosmic killjoy. Don't let them have the impression that your love and devotion to him has made you miserable. Don't quiet your laughter or discard your flowers. Don't be so somber and solemn. Don't dress or act like you're on your way to a funeral. Don't let all of your songs be sung in a minor chord. If you do, you will play into the world's mistaken idea and bring reproach on your Lord."

Think about it: is it consistent to look nice and dress nice? Are those who do the ones who are despondent and depressed—who think that they will perish at any moment? No, to dress happy and act happy is only justified by those who fervently believe in the reality of the resurrection. Which is more consistent for those who know the Lord: to sit alone, downtrodden and downcast, or to thoroughly enjoy every passing hour? I think that it is more consistent for those who believe in eternal life than for those who believe that once the hour is past, it can never be regained. Lost joys should never cause us to be sad because half of every pleasure is found in the hope that it will last. Who enjoys the little things in life more? Those who think that they are passing or those who see the simple pleasures as eternal? I believe that it is those who know that our God takes great delight in even the smallest things of life. Who takes great pleasure—basks, even—in human love? Is it those who see love as simply chemical reactions in the human brain or those who know love to be a chief attribute of the person of God, one that He builds into His highest creation?

I believe that the Psalmist is correct. I believe that those who truly trust in the Lord are allowed to experience a higher happiness, a fuller joy, than those who don't know Him. No doubt, the world has, like Adam, stolen the Lord's apples and placed them under its own tree. The world has claimed happiness as its own. It has claimed both the Tree of Life and the Tree of Knowledge. The rivers and mountains, beauty and poetry, happiness and revelry have been relegated to man's dominion. But the Scripture tells us to enter into the joy of our Lord, and I believe that the Lord's joy also includes man's joy.

There are many Christians who try to show that they are the Lord's by displaying their toils and tears, but the Psalmist commands, "…let all those rejoice who put their trust in You; Let them ever shout for joy…" How can we ever seek to bring the world into the beauty of the Lord's love when we are seen as standing in the shadows or wallowing in our own despair? Will the world truly believe in our Lord's love if we sail on ships with flags flown at half-mast? If we wear the black robes of mourning, won't the world rightly say of us, "These are they who are even now in great tribulation"? We must not be adorned so. Those of us who have been delivered from the far country should be dressed in the best, brightest, most brilliant of garments. We should be covered in our Father's jewels, greeted with a feast, surrounded with the music and dancing of the Father's house. We should teach those who don't know our great God that for those who are redeemed, it is good to make merry and be glad!

Thoughts

_____

_____

_____

_____

_____

_____

_____

_____

_____

_____

18

Fit for Glory

By faith Enoch was taken away so that he did not see death, and was not found, because God had taken him; for before he was taken he had this testimony, that he pleased God. Hebrews 11:5

Doesn't the end of this verse seem to be a bit anticlimactic? Think about it. The writer of Hebrews tells us that Enoch was taken—translated "raptured"—to Heaven, and what a truly tremendous revelation that is. But for the writer of Hebrews to then add to such an amazing account the fact that before Enoch was taken "he had this testimony, that he pleased God" is no doubt evident and expected. In fact, one could easily say, "Well that makes sense; he got to go to the place of God so surely it is unnecessary to say he had pleased the person of God." Well, actually it isn't superfluous at all. In fact, it is the one thing that is necessary to finish such a fantastic picture.

You see, today we talk about being raptured to Heaven as if that is the only thing that would be needed to make us happy. When, in reality, it wouldn't make us happy at all, unless before we were taken the joy of Heaven was already in our hearts. For me to meet God—come face to face with Him—wouldn't be a happy or joyous time if I had not already received the Spirit of God.

If I were invited to spend an afternoon with somebody who was imminently educated, a genius even, in some art or field of study, would that be a source of joy in my soul? It all depends on whether or not I was prepared to be in their presence. To sit and talk with some world-renowned poet would be torture if I were not a poet at heart. To have lunch with a world-famous musician wouldn't be fun at all if there were not a song in my heart. So to be raptured to glory would be pure misery if the Spirit of Heaven was not already in my soul. You see, I must first know the mind of Christ before I can truly rejoice in the sight of God.

Do you think that it would make you happy to be raptured up to Heaven today? Don't answer too quickly. Take a moment to really consider your response and the implications. Ask yourself, "Am I already in sympathy with the joys of Heaven?" If there is not already Heaven in your heart, then how in the world is simply changing locations going to make any difference at all? If you are not already heavenly minded, then how could a fiery chariot ride cause your thoughts to become so? You see, there is something more that is necessary if your rapture is to make a joyful difference in your soul. You must come to know the One beyond death on this side of death. There must be a relationship with the One who is "the Way, the Truth and the Life" before you leave this life if eternity is to be a happy, joyful place for you.

> *Lord, take those things which are Yours and show them to me. Help me to learn to love them while I am on this side of the Valley of the Shadow of Death. I don't want to meet them and see them as some sort of strange objects of a foreign land. Teach me while I am here the elementary, essential lessons of Heaven. Let pleasing You here become my pleasure. May serving You now be my freedom, and knowing You more today be my life. May beholding Your*

beauty inspire me to seek You even more. Show me the joy of Your salvation so that the place of Your salvation would not be a source of pain. This is the testimony I ask before I am taken. Amen.

Thoughts

19

When We Need His Armor the Most

Therefore take up the whole armor of God, that you may be able to withstand in the evil day, and having done all, to stand.
Ephesians 6:13

This seems to be a very odd ending to such a blatant battle cry. Normally the soldier is told to gear up, get ready for the battle by putting on his armor, but here he's told to gear up to do nothing more than stay back in the camp. This seems to be a very strange statement. One would naturally consider the hard part of the Christian life to be the day of battle, the hour of the conflict. Paul, however, takes a different view. He sees the difficult day, the time of testing, to be that which comes after the fight has ended.

If we were to write this passage, we would probably write something like, "Therefore put on the whole armor of God, and stand ready to face your foe, so that when the evil day is over you will have defeated your enemy." However, Paul says the exact opposite. Paul says that the hardest part is not the fighting, but the resting. He sees the greatest danger as coming when the Christian has "done all"—and Paul is right!

The hardest part of the Christian life isn't found in the field, but in the barracks. You see, in the heat of battle, when we're surrounded by so great a cloud of witnesses, it is much easier to lay aside those things that weigh us down. But when the battle has ended and all is quiet, when there is no longer a foe to fight or a wreath to win, when the battlefield is our heart and our foe our own desires, when there is no human voice to shout "Well done!" and no audience to say "He fought a good fight!"—that is the time when our armor is needed the most.

That's why I pray that the Lord will equip and strengthen me for the quiet times when I'm all alone by myself. So many times I find that when the hour of battle comes I am brave, but when it is over I am weak. As a pastor, I see this lived out in the lives of those who have recently lost a loved one. There are the hours when they have to be strong. There are friends and family to speak to, a service to be arranged and attended. There are letters to write and words of appreciation to give. Many people drop in to share their love and a word of encouragement. A brave, strong face is presented to all, but when everybody is gone and they are all alone there is a cry that comes from deep inside, begging the Lord to save them from themselves. They petition the Lord to guard them from the loneliness of their own heart and equip them to stand against themselves.

How many times have I been bold and brave in the middle of the battle because I heard the cries of my companions? How many times have I pressed forward because of the encouragement and sympathy of my brothers in arms? Don't I need those same cries even more in the middle of my night's watch? The day's work is much easier because there is something to do. But what about at night, when I'm alone in the shadows, and there is no work that can be done?

We must learn that the heart has an even greater work than the hand. We must realize that we are not only soldiers when we are in the midst of the battle, and that courage that can endure is far greater than that which can only strike. Thus, there is a greater heroism to be found in Gethsemane than is even found at Calvary, for it was alone in the Garden that Jesus took the weight that only He could bear and set His face to finish the work that only He could do.

My Lord has armed me with a sword for the conflict, but He has also equipped me with a breastplate for when all is calm. Thus, my armor will only be complete when I, having done all, can simply stand.

Thoughts

_____

_____

_____

_____

_____

_____

_____

_____

_____

_____

20

Why God Hides His Face

He covers the face of His throne, And spreads His cloud over it.
Job 26:9

What a startling statement. God Himself hides His sovereignty. Now I can understand why God would hide His beauty, because any picture is made up of both light strokes and dark strokes. It even makes sense that He would hide His plans and purposes because in our finite, ignorant minds, we might not understand the benefit found in them. But what sense is to be found in the hiding of His sovereignty?

The most startling aspect of this statement is the deliberate nature of God's veiling. If this verse simply said that the mind of man cannot understand the mind of God—that His thoughts are higher than our thoughts—then we would certainly agree with the truth of that statement. But it is God who describes and determines the truth of His unfathomableness. In fact, there are two acts that the Almighty uses to describe His concealment. At first "He covers the face of His throne." Then He "spreads His cloud over it." It is an intricate act of veiling, and it bothers us.

What is it, then, that is actually veiled? Is it the throne of God that is veiled? No, it is only "the face of His throne." What is "the face of His throne"? It is that which looks forward. It is the sovereignty of God that is seen in advance, and He says that He will not unveil that. He will unveil the side of His throne giving strength for our present need. He will unveil the back of His throne, allowing us to see His working in retrospect. But He will not unveil for us the face of His throne. In fact, He spreads a cloud over that future glory.

What a benefit and blessing. My Father doesn't force me to come to Him. He wants me to come because of love, by my own free will. That's why He covers the face of His throne and spreads a cloud over it. He does this for our good, for what man could resist such glory? What man would be able to refuse the face of God? To see such a vision would no doubt rob man of his freedom. Who wouldn't climb God's holy hill if it were always crowned with light? For if there is too much light, then there is no way that our love could be tested or even offered.

It's easy to seek God when we see the emerald shimmering and the sapphire blazing in His rainbow. But what would happen if the rainbow were removed, the sapphire stopped blazing, and the emerald ceased to shimmer? What if the face of His throne were concealed, covered by a cloud? Would we still seek Him? If Heaven announced that there would be no judgment seat, the books would not be open and there would be no dividing to the right hand and the left, would virtue still be as beautiful to you? Would you choose her if she were so plainly clothed? Would you love her if she were not wearing His adoption ring? Would you marry her without any material dowry? Would you hold and cherish her knowing that there would be no hope of reward? Would you work for her, labor for her, sacrifice for her if you were never to hear the words uttered, "Well done, good and faithful servant"? If so, then the silence from Heaven's throne is vindicated, and you may thank your Father that He has hidden the face of His throne from you.

Thoughts

_____

_____

_____

_____

21

The Lord's Use of Adversity

What profit is it that we…have walked as mourners Before the LORD of hosts? Malachi 3:14

What profit is there in walking mournfully? None. The only thing that truly profits a man is joy. You see, the advantage to sorrow's fire is not found in the things that are consumed, but rather in those things that it cannot consume. So the best and most beneficial use of adversity is for it to reveal the one thing that it cannot take way—my joy.

There's a material that fire cannot destroy, much like the burning bush that Moses encountered in the desert. The only way for the substance of that shrub to be proved was by the fire. But don't misunderstand; the blessing is not found in the burning or what was being burnt up, but rather in what was not.

The three Hebrew Children—Shadrach, Meshach, and Abednego—walked through the fiery furnace and remained unsinged. In fact, they didn't even smell like smoke. So what, then, was the purpose of passing through the fire? It was to show what the furnace couldn't do, to demonstrate the limitations of its fiery power. I'm sure inconsequential things were tossed into the fire that were immediately consumed. In fact, that's what Daniel records for us. Those three young men were thrown in bound and came out of the fire loosed. But as great a miracle and act of deliverance as that was, it is not the thing that makes the fire so beneficial. What makes the furnace so fantastic is what it left untouched, unsinged, unharmed. The ultimate glory of that furnace is found in what it failed to do.

The ultimate glory of sorrow is very similar. Sorrow finds it glory in that which it cannot accomplish, what it fails to do. Sometimes as believers we think that our grief is somehow pleasing to our Heavenly Father. In reality, there is nothing that pleases our Father more than our joy. He doesn't search our hearts looking to find our pain, but rather our pearl. He desires to see the tenacity of our joyfulness—to see that it refuses to be extinguished.

Was Jesus the Father's Beloved because He was "a Man of sorrows and acquainted with grief"? No, but rather because even all the sorrows He suffered could not extinguish His joy. It was for the joy that was set before Him that He endured the cross and despised the shame. In fact, even under the cross' shadow, our Savior said, "My peace I give to you…" It was that peace, not His pain, that was the Father's pearl. It was not His cloud but the rainbow in the cloud that made His Father's heart rejoice. The same is true in our lives today.

Why does the Father send clouds into our lives? To defeat us? To demoralize us? To make us depressed? No, it is to test the tenacity of our joy. To see whether the rainbow can be seen in the flood or the dove can live on the waters. Why would He send cypress when what He seeks for is the laurel? Why sing a funeral dirge when He's asked for a song of praise? The Lord blocks the sun not so that you can see the night but so that you can see your candle—the source of internal joy. He is gratified in the carrying of your grief because the only thing that can truly bear it is your joy. That's why the fires of your life are never turned to cleansing until the gleam and glitter of gold becomes visible.

Thoughts

_____

_____

_____

_____

22

The Place of Penalty's Pardon

Esau…found no place for repentance, though he sought it diligently with tears. Hebrews 12:16–17

The writer of Hebrews isn't saying what you might think at first glance. He's not saying that Esau found no repentance. He says that Esau found no *place* of repentance. His repentance was evident, and as a result so was his forgiveness. What this verse teaches us is that his repentance did not restore the position he lost in his community.

It is possible to experience the forgiveness of Heaven and not be restored by men. Consider the fact that David was pardoned and then received his punishment. You say, "That is troubling." No, it is comforting because there are times when we are overtaken by the just penalty of our actions and think that it's the result of Heaven's anger. That may not be the case. You may have already been forgiven. You see, when you seek forgiveness "carefully and with tears," you will receive it instantly, completely, and finally.

The Father has prepared a place of forgiveness for the repentant in His heavenly home, but such a place may not necessarily be found here on Earth. The younger son wasted all of his inheritance on prodigal living. Then he heard the voice of the father and returned home. However, his return did not restore the inheritance he had wasted in the far country. Sure, we're told that there was a ring and a robe that awaited his return. In fact, it was the best ring and the best robe, but it wasn't his old ring or his old robe. He had wasted and lost his prior position. His father will raise him up and give him a new estate, but it will not be the former one. Thus, he returns home in rags and want. It is a poor, malnourished man who listens that night to the music and dancing. He has been welcomed, but he's received nothing more. He hears the song while still feeling the thorn. He has been hugged and kissed by the father, but the harvest he sowed still remains.

I am comforted and strengthened by the story of the prodigal, for here I learn that the Father's pardon may precede my peace. What an encouragement when I am not at peace. When the answers to my cries of forgiveness seem only to be the results of my wandering way, it is helpful to remember that the prodigal was welcomed home long before his glory was restored. When I find myself fallen from the estate of men; when I walk home wearing nothing but rags; when I reap the harvest of my own sinful sowing, I must remember that the prodigal was embraced before he was exalted.

I'm thankful to my Lord that His pardon doesn't have to wait for my peace. His forgiveness doesn't sit by the wayside. His mercy toward me isn't dependent on the mercy of men. The repentant thief reaped the results of his lawless deeds, but the One in the middle didn't wait for the law to run its course. The cross may crucify him, but not before Christ crowns him. Earth will close behind him, but not before Heaven's gates open before him. His birthright is lost, but His kingdom comes first and even before the place knows him no more, Jesus has prepared a place in paradise for him.

Thoughts

_____

_____

_____

_____

23

Alone with Jesus

Then those who heard it, being convicted by their conscience, went out one by one, beginning with the oldest even to the last. And Jesus was left alone, and the woman standing in the midst. John 8:9

What a picture of the Day of Judgment. A single, sinful soul has a face-to-face encounter with Jesus as her judge. Those who had condemned her slowly left one by one until she was left all alone with the Lord.

I believe that is a type of Jesus' judgment of all souls. I think that after death there will be a meeting, a moment of solitude where the spirit of man will stand face to face with Jesus. I believe that it will be a moment of simple reflection and solemn review in which the past will be as present. I will see myself as I really am in the light of the Son of Man.

You say, "I thought that it was going to be a general review with everybody standing there as one big group. In fact, doesn't the Bible teach that the small and great will stand before God?" Yes, but that doesn't mean that they're going to stand before you or you before them. You may very well be in a line—a procession—where everyone is so consumed with their own shortcomings and sin that those around them seem invisible. Now, God surely sees it all, but you may well be only conscious of the fact that you are standing before Him. You may not hear the steps behind or even see the one in front of you. You very likely will feel yourself all alone with God.

I think this moment of review and reflection is much better suited for self-examination than perhaps the option. You see, the presence—or awareness—of many others may actually cause me to not examine my life in the light of the Son of Man, but rather in the light of other men. The crowd could very well become a contrary influence for it makes me look out, not in. It causes me to criticize the choices and actions of those around me, instead of considering my life in the light of my Lord. I would probably be like Peter, who instead of asking forgiveness for his denial of Jesus, looked at John and asked, "Lord, what about him?" That's why it's a good thing that there should be a time where everybody else is shut out, when John is hidden from Peter's view. It is good that there will be a moment on that mount when I will see no man but Jesus.

Practice being alone with Jesus. Mark tells us in his gospel that "… when they were alone, He explained all things to His disciples." That was not only true in their lives; it is true in ours, as well. If you really want to see yourself, understand yourself, then you will have to send the multitude away. Let them all leave one by one, like the men in John 8, until you are left standing there alone with Christ. To be alone with Him is in essence to having your judgment day, for it was only when Jesus got rid of the Pharisees that the woman began to feel her own sinfulness. As long as they lingered, she could excuse herself by saying, "They're just as bad as I am." But when the Pharisees finally left, she lost the ability to point at them and had to deal with her own condition. She stood all alone in the Lord's court with the Lord of the court, and she could only measure her life by His.

Have you ever imagined that you were the only person left on Earth? That everybody else was gone and you were the only living creature left in all of creation? In such a world, your every thought would be, "It's just God and me. Me and God!" The reality of that truth is much nearer than we often realize. He is just as near to you now as if the only hearts that beat in all of the universe were yours and His.

Christian, practice solitude. Practice the putting out of the crowd. Practice the secret of stilling your own heart and standing alone in His presence. Learn the truth of the solemn, simple refrain, "It's just God and me. Me and God!" Don't let anybody come between you and your wrestling angel. You will be both condemned and pardoned when you come face to face with Christ alone.

Thoughts

24

The Light of the Lord's Life

In Him was life, and the life was the light of men. John 1:4

The light of Jesus has illumined the entire world, not by what He has done, but by what He was—"His life was the light of men." We often speak of the "life's work" of a man, but Jesus' life's work was His life.

When I want to get light from other men, I read their books or listen to their words, but when I want to get light from Jesus, I simply look to Him. As odd as it might sound, it is not so much what He says that I treasure—as great as that is—I treasure Him. You see, the Sermon on the Mount is amazing, but the sermon's Preacher is even more amazing.

Some say that the first Easter morning revealed Jesus' glory, but I believe the opposite to be true. I believe that it was His glory that actually revealed the first Easter morning. It's not the resurrection that made Jesus; it is Jesus who has made the resurrection. For those who have seen His beauty, even the Mount of Olives can do nothing to add to their conviction. The light of immortality is just as bright on His cross as it is on His crown.

Jesus said of Himself, "I *am* the resurrection and the life." He didn't say, "I teach the resurrection" or "I bring about the resurrection" or "I predict that there will be a resurrection." He said, "I am." For Him, it was almost beside the point to say, "In my Father's house are many mansions," because His life should be enough light all by itself. That's why He said, "If it were not so, I would have told you."

Do you worry about tomorrow or fret about the future? Are you looking for proof of Jesus among the stars of the sky or even the angels of Heaven? If so, you're looking too far. It is His life, not His works, that will be your light.

What proves that spring has arrived? Is it the buds or the blossoms? Is it the birds or the bees? No, it is the warmth of the sun on your face and the fresh breath in your lungs. That's why no man can find the pearly gates that lead to everlasting life simply by searching. There is no way through those gates except through the one who claimed to be "the way, the truth, and the life." It is through His life that we have life. So do you find that the pearly gates are dim to your sight? Don't attempt to adjust your focus. Forget about the gate and look on Him because He is the door, He is the way, and He is the light of life.

Thoughts

25

My Father's Hidden Hand

*His brightness was like the light; He had rays flashing from His hand,
And there His power was hidden. Habakkuk 3:4*

What an amazing and yet completely reassuring thought—my Father hides His omnipotence for my benefit. It is surely the most fantastic fiction ever conceived, for it allows me to have freedom of will. He loves me so much that He puts me in the wilderness and tells me to walk alone, but He never leaves my side. He continues to walk beside me, holding on to the hem of my garment. He hides the loving guidance of His omnipotent hand, making it appear as if He were not there. He stands afar off and says to me, "Come." He allows me to think that I am all by myself. He doesn't let me see His everlasting arms that surround me. He doesn't let me feel the care that envelopes me should I ever dash my foot upon a rock. He conceals the truth that I am totally, utterly, and jealously guarded on all sides. He hides His supporting arm in the mist, leaving margin for my personal choice.

If the fire is needed in the darkness of the night, the cloud is needed that much more in the light of the day. If I were to see the undimmed brilliance of His omnipotence, it would destroy my humanity—the height of His creation—and force me to come. However, I must not be forced to come. I must come of my own free will. I must not be driven from the forbidden fruit by a cherub with a fiery sword. The stars of His creation are driven—they are compelled to give light. But I'm not a star in the sky; I'm a soul, so I must not be coerced. I must choose to love Him because coerced love is no love at all. That's why God hides Himself among the trees of the garden: so that I may feel that I am free. This is why I am so glad that my Father has not completely and totally revealed Himself to me. This is why I'm glad that He not only gives the rainbow, but also the cloud.

So often men praise my Father for His many powerful voices, but we ought to also praise Him for His silence, too. His silence is precious and powerful, for it gives voice to my heart. In the silence my heart sings, my faith soars, my imagination speeds, my hope sees, my conscience seeks, and my will finds space to love and follow Him. His silence is my song. His shadow shows so much. His night is my light. When I don't feel His hand of judgment, I realize the majesty of simply coming because I love Him. It is when I don't hear the sound of His last trumpet that I can listen to the still, small voice of judgment deep within. When the thunders of Sinai have ceased, there is found room for the sighing of my soul's love. This is why I am so thankful that my Father has hidden the fullness of His power—for now.

Thoughts

26

The Curse of Indifference

Woe to you who are at ease in Zion... Amos 6:1

I believe that the saddest thing in the world is indifference. I think that it is sadder than any heresy, sadder than any false belief; yes, sadder even than any honest unbelief.

You see, the mind that has struggled into rest is one to be envied. The mind that has struggled without ever finding rest has to be appreciated. But the mind that has never even experienced any struggle at all, well, that mind is to be pitied.

The Revelator says that a man had better be either hot or cold. I believe that he's exactly right. I can comprehend a man looking at the Creator's creation and believing. I can somewhat understand a man looking at the Creator's creation and doubting. What I cannot understand is a man who won't even raise his head to look at the Creator's creation.

Wonder that turns into worship is natural. Wonder that leads to skepticism is perhaps possible. But that a mind can exist without wonder is, to me, inconceivable. It can only be explained by a fundamental lack—some sort of deficiency in the mind itself.

If, then, indifference is the saddest of all things, then it is sadder still when it occurs in the midst of serious circumstances. To be at ease, for a mind, is never a noble or desirable thing, but for a mind to be "at ease in Zion" is a terrible tragedy! It's like someone laughing out in the middle of a funeral. It's like a daughter dancing around the grave of her father.

Being flippant really is a sad spectacle at any time, but being flippant in the presence of greatness is especially sad. To be flippant in the middle of a national tragedy, to be flippant during national victory, to be flippant when the days are dark and dreadful, to be flippant in the light of love, to be flippant when the glory or shadow of God is passing by—that is truly tragic. It really means to be less than a man. That's what it means to be "at ease in Zion."

So many times I worry about and lament the fact that this human soul of mine seems to be the most burdened of any creature in God's creation. I often compare the care I carry to others in the Creator's creation—and then I find myself worrying even more. I consider the cardinal's carol or the swallow's song and I wonder what is wrong with me, but then He shows me that my burden is in fact my glory. I find that I am not "at ease in Zion" simply because I am "in Zion." The shadow that dims my sight is His shadow. The weight that weighs down my wings is my ever-present sense of Him.

I'm learning that if I weren't my brother's keeper, then I might be like the birds and have an unending, enduring song on my lips. But there is no way I can divest myself of that responsibility. In fact, I don't think my God would have me be any other way. I would rather walk in the shade with my God than to soar with the bird in the light. My care is considerably better than a carol. My sigh is substantially more significant than a song. I have seen the King in all of His beauty. I have heard Heaven's music from afar, and therefore the discords of this world grate on my ears. I have seen His spotless robe, and therefore my brother's rags break my heart. His rainbow brings my flood.

I know that it is hard to comprehend, but it is the Lord's beauty that brings my burden, His glory that lends to my gloom, His nearness that brings my night. Why shouldn't I take His yoke upon me? Should I refuse to suffer the pain that His children alone can feel? Should I reject the weight of the heart that comes only to those on whom He has laid His hand? No, I would rather live and move and find my being in Him and bear His shadows in my soul. You see, to lose the lark's ease, the cardinal's carol, is simply the price that I pay for being in Zion.

Thoughts

27

The Goodness of God's Spirit

*Teach me to do Your will, For You are my God; Your Spirit is good.
Lead me in the land of uprightness. Psalm 143:10*

What a striking contrast between the Psalmist's prayer and that of the Muslim. The Muslim prays "Teach me your will," and "lead me to a destined land," but that's where the similarity ends. The Muslim wants to be taught the will of his god because he believes it is his destiny. The Psalmist desires to be taught God's will because it is good. You see, unlike the Muslim, the Psalmist doesn't view the will of God as an arbitrary, capricious thing that comes and goes with every passing hour. The Psalmist realizes that it is the voice of One who has no choice but righteousness. It is His nature—who He is. Thus, the Psalmist declares "Your Spirit is good."

The Psalmist wouldn't say "Your will be done" to just any object of worship because it isn't simply a will that he reverences; it's the power behind the will—the Spirit. He wouldn't allow himself to be led simply by blind fate that doesn't know where it's going or how it will get there. He gives no value to submission simply for the sake of submission. What he desires is submission to that which is right. He will only obey such will that comes from a "good spirit," and since it comes from a good spirit it leads to a land of righteousness.

My prayer is that as a follower of Jesus I can wholeheartedly, unreservedly say, "Your will be done." The Muslim no doubt says something similar to his god. So who am I to resist the decrees of the Lord or refuse to submit to His mandates? It isn't in my nature to willingly bend, but unlike the Muslim's god, my God doesn't wish for me to bend to His unrelenting force. He wouldn't have me accept His will because I must, but rather because I may. My God wouldn't have me take it with reservation; He wants me to receive it with joy, not simply without complaint but with praise.

So how can I reach such a godly goal? I can only do so by understanding what the Psalmist understood—that the will of God comes from His good spirit and leads to a land of righteousness. His will is loving and wise. He doesn't lead me wearing a blindfold, but with my eyes wide open. He gives me the power to look behind and ahead—behind me to His good Spirit and ahead to His land of righteousness.

Blessed is the man whose delight is in the law of the Lord. Who can tell of His statutes with a heart of rejoicing? He will obey God's will in perfect freedom because He can honestly, openly say, "Your Spirit is good."

Thoughts

28

The Strength of the Savior's Sacrifice

Therefore My Father loves Me, because I lay down My life that I may take it again. No one takes it from Me, but I lay it down of Myself. I have power to lay it down, and I have power to take it again. This command I have received from My Father. John 10:17–18

Here Jesus shares a heavenly secret. He speaks of the Father's love for Him, but what is the secret that the Savior shares with us? Why does the heart of the Father rejoice in the Son? Was it because of the suffering of the Son? Was it because the Father saw Him as a helpless victim on death's altar? Not at all. It is because when Jesus was being offered as the perfect sacrifice for all sin, for all people, for all time, He was anything except a victim. The heart of the Father didn't rejoice in the fact that the Son was forced to die, but rather because the Son was willing to die without being forced. In fact, Jesus states unequivocally that He has the unparalleled power to actually lay down His life.

You see, every other type of sacrifice has been a picture of weakness, but the death of Jesus was unique in that it is a picture of power. In fact, His death shows us strength of will that has never been seen in such glory. Sure, there have been great warriors and mighty conquerors who have paved their own way through the hearts of others, but here was One who paved a path for others through His own heart.

Never has there been presented such a perfect and powerful presentation of love as that which Jesus demonstrated for us on the cross. If He had simply resigned Himself to death, we could admire Him. If He had so despised life, we could pity Him. However, since He willingly chose to die for us because of His great love, we love Him. We magnify the strength that could surrender strength, the power that could abandon power, the might that could relinquish might, the will that could resign will. That's why He is crowned for us in what was the valley of His humiliation. He is most glorious to us in the shadows of Gethsemane.

He was not a victim of Golgotha, for nails could not have kept Him on the cross if love had not held Him there. He willingly chose the cross. That's why twelve legions of angels could not have caused Him to climb down from Calvary's height. That's why His cross is not a picture of weakness but of power. We are not to be ashamed of it—we are to glory in it. We as Christ-followers are to long to be made conformable unto His death, to crucify our wills and dreams and desires. We are to look on Him until His death so imprints our lives and we are transformed from glory to glory. Then we will say, not with hesitant resignation but with complete and confident assurance, "Your will be done."

Thoughts

_____

_____

_____

_____

_____

29

Temptation's Location

And He was there in the wilderness forty days, tempted by Satan, and was with the wild beasts; and the angels ministered to Him. Mark 1:13

"He was there in the wilderness…tempted by Satan." Many times we are tempted to believe that Satan is the strongest in the busiest and most crowded areas of our lives. Those areas where we find the greatest number of people and opportunities to sin. That is a fatal mistake. I believe that the greatest location of temptation is not in the hustle and bustle of a crowd, but in the stillness and quietness of the wilderness.

This truth is seen repeatedly in the pages of Scripture. It is not in their hours of public service that the powerful men of the past have fallen; rather, it has been in the quietest hours of their personal life.

Think about Moses. He never wavered or stumbled while he was standing before and speaking to Pharaoh. He never fell even as he was fleeing from Pharaoh and his army. No, it was out in the desert, when he was tired and impatient, that he finally fell.

Think of David. He never stumbled in the days when he was fighting his way through the forces of his enemies. Rather, it was after the battle was over, when he was safe and secure—resting within the walls of his own palace—that he reached out and took that which wasn't his.

The greatest temptations are not those that are the loudest spoken, but those with the softest echo. It is far easier to put aside your besetting sin in the midst of a cloud of witnesses than in the privacy of your own room. That sin that besets you is never so besetting as when you are by yourself. You may speak kindly and graciously to that man that you hate when you see him in public but make up for it when you are all alone. You see, it is our own thoughts that do the most damage, and we tend to do most of our thinking when we are alone with ourselves.

Paul says that we are never so vulnerable, we never have a greater need for our spiritual armor, than when we have defeated our outward enemy. He tells us in Ephesians 6:13 to "… take up the whole armor of God, that you may be able to withstand in the evil day, and having done all, to stand."

That's where I most need the Lord's help with my thoughts—in the wilderness. Others can help me in the city square. Others can give me counsel at a time of celebration. Others can intervene in the meetings of a multitude. But only He can help me in my wilderness. That is where I most need His strength.

I have lived my life trying to be separated from the temptations of life, but I find when I relax, when I rest, that is when the temptations of life most often come to my mind. Temptation resides in my own soul. It is an artist who paints in my own heart. It is not when I go to celebrate a wedding in Cana that I most need my Lord, but rather when I hear music and dancing and, because I'm jealous of my brother, I refuse to go in. That is my wilderness moment—when I cut myself off from the strength of other believers.

That's why I ask the Lord to meet me in my moments of temptation. I ask Him to meet with me when I cut myself off from those around me. When I lose the voices of the crowd, when I begin to walk in the wilderness—alone. That is when I need His strength the most. It is there, when He is with me, that He will break the worldliness of the wilderness in my own heart.

Thoughts

_____

_____

_____

30

The Gift of a Thorn

And lest I should be exalted above measure by the abundance of the revelations, a thorn in the flesh was given to me, a messenger of Satan to buffet me, lest I be exalted above measure. 2 Corinthians 12:7

"A thorn…was given to me." So was this thorn then a gift from God? I normally view as gifts from God those things in which the abundance of life is found. If something happens to diminish or dilute that abundance, I definitely don't consider it a gift. At best, I consider it to be a distraction—at worst, a danger. But here in Paul's personal letter to the Christians at Corinth, he completely reverses that which was my understanding. He says that the danger is the gift—the thorn is the abundance.

Paul had been exalted in a singularly special way. He had been blessed by God to see sights, hear sounds, and experience that which nobody else ever has. In fact, his entire life had been a great big bouquet of flowers. Thus, God sent a thorn among the flowers for the benefit of his soul.

"But how can a thorn be a blessing?" you ask. Because there is something special, protective even, about a thorn. It's certainly not something pleasant to look upon. There's no sweet fragrance like there is with the petal. Yet the thorn still proves to be a special gift to my human heart in that it reminds me that I am still human.

It was a startling realization—I had never really stopped to thank my God for the gift of the thorn. I had often thanked Him for the bouquet of flowers but never for the thorn. I had thanked Him that one day I would receive compensation for carrying my cross, but I had never stopped to consider that my cross is its own current compensation.

The Lord allowed me to learn the triumph of the thorn, the value of suffering, the glory of my cross. He showed me that it was through the path of pain that I have drawn closer to Him. I was allowed to see that it is my tears that have provided my rainbow. He taught me that it was through wrestling with Him until the break of day that I have been strengthened. Then I realized that my thorn was indeed a gift from above. I have celebrated the hour of my sorrow and have marked that monument with the words, "It is good for me that I have been afflicted, that I may learn Your statutes."

Thoughts

_____

_____

_____

_____

_____

_____

_____

_____

31

Sacrifice at Sunset

Now it came to pass after these things that God tested Abraham, and said to him, "Abraham!" And he said, "Here I am." Genesis 22:1

After these things..." After what things? After all the things of Abraham's life. Isn't that a strange place to assign such a sacrificial test? Normally we would expect that a man would be tested in the beginning of his life—in the years when the sun is rising. Why, then, is Abraham subjected to such a sacrificial test at sunset? Why has the sacrificial hour been placed at the close of his life? Isn't it normally expected that such a test would come in the time when a man's power of sacrifice would be the most accurate measure of him? The simple answer is "No. No it's not."

No doubt, that is the time of life when we hear the most about sacrifice. Young people are the ones who most often nurture the melancholy, who often devise for themselves terrific plans of self-sacrifice. But not much value is placed on the sacrifices of youth. Why is that? Because most feel that they are willing to give up that which they have never tasted.

You see, life doesn't reveal its true beauty at the threshold. Life's true beauty is only found after you've climbed the stairs. Youth's romance is really just its search for another world. That's why romance dies after life—because that's when the things that are real become precious. So it's only when those things have become precious that the life of sacrifice is truly a life of unselfishness. The transfiguration must come before the cross. The gift that you give must first be dear to you before it can become sweet to its recipient. Before God tests Abraham, He must appeal to the joy of Abraham's heart: "Your son whom you love."

Such was the Savior's sacrifice. The life that He gave for me was not one that would have been considered light or inconsequential. His was not the pessimistic offering of a melancholy youth. It was not the giving of a withered and dried flower. He didn't offer Himself to be rid of a barren world. He didn't depart the earth because He no longer found joy in the beauty of His creation. He was crowned with glory and honor for His sacrifice.

The life that He willingly gave up was one of great beauty. He recognized its beauty and enjoyed it. He had tasted and enjoyed every pure delight before He was called to lay His life down. He had sat with the wise in the temple. He had ministered to friends at a wedding. He had watched as the children played. He had enjoyed the fellowship of friends. He had felt the warmth and love of family. He had experienced the value of human devotion. Every good door of life had been opened to Him. So it wasn't because life was poor or not worth living that He climbed the cross and willingly sacrificed Himself. He climbed and He died because of His great love for me.

That's why I would climb and offer myself for Him—for love. I wouldn't seek Heaven because I despised Earth; I would bring the treasures of this world with me. I would not wing my way to Him in my heart's winter. I desire to come while the green grass and lush leaves of summer remain. I would come with a blooming rose, a ripe fruit, the sweetest songs of the day. I would willingly break my alabaster box when it was full, not when it is empty. Thus, my sacrifice would be a sacrifice of praise.

Thoughts

_____

_____

_____

32

The Light of Life

Then Jesus spoke to them again, saying, "I am the light of the world. He who follows Me shall not walk in darkness, but have the light of life."
John 8:12

No light in all the world is so beautiful as the light of life. No light is so revealing, either. Nature's light doesn't tell us half as much as we'd like to know. In fact, there is a greater revelation in the faintest breath of life than in the strongest tremors of the brightest stars. The helpless cry of a baby has more to say to the human heart than the noonday sun in all of its strength. Life's light carries in its very being all possible revelations, for it reveals both my God and my immortality. All arguments for the existence of my God pale in comparison before this certainty, and all arguments for my immortality fail in the brilliance of immortality begun. Life is like Jacob's ladder, reaching from Earth to Heaven and binding the two. The smallest spark of life is the very first ascending step whose midpoint is the angel and whose summit is God's own throne. The more life that is in me, the closer I am to His Throne. My revelation doesn't grow from what I receive from without, but rather from what I gain from within. Doesn't the scripture say, "And this is eternal life, that they may know You, the only true God..."? How marvelous is that? That I can have this unbelievable glory—here and now, in this world. "He who follows Me shall not walk in darkness, but have the light of life." It won't come to me by dying, but by following—following the steps of Jesus through His straight gate and narrow path. It's by taking up the cross, lifting the burden, bearing the sacrifice, doing His will that I can know this truth.

Have you measured the true value of your life? It's not found in its leading but in its following. It's not what you have that reveals to you your immortality—it's the sense of what you don't have. Your measure is found in your aspiration, in your thirst for Jesus. Everything rises to its own level. If your goal were dust, then you wouldn't seek to be anything more than dust. As long as you are a child of the dust, then the dust would satisfy you. It is the smallness of your life that makes you so. But as your life grows, it looks for more than it can get down here below. It seeks the measure of the perfect Man—His fullness that fills all in all. Your glory is your power to follow; it says to you that there is something beyond, bigger than you that is yet your birthright. Your cry for God is His voice within you. Your longing for Heaven's air is the breath of Heaven in your heart. Your conscious desire is your open door. Your sense of sin is your Pisgah's height. And your vision of the world's growing shadow is made by the light of eternal life.

Thoughts

_____

_____

_____

_____

_____

33

The Shield of Sacrifice

Therefore, since Christ suffered for us in the flesh, arm yourselves also with the same mind… 1 Peter 4:1

The context is considerable. These words were spoken in the middle of a military empire. They were delivered to a people who were disciplined in the use of weapons as a way of life. It must have been startling, then, to hear these words from Peter. It was the promise of a new kind of armor, a new type of defense. It must have caught them off guard and left them flatfooted. Then they must have laughed. There was nothing tangible to it. It wasn't tall and skinny, short and fat, lightweight or heavy. It couldn't cause the first wound on the most elementary enemy. It was, in fact, a wound itself.

"Therefore, since Christ suffered for us in the flesh, arm yourselves also with the same mind…" Now, as believers, we can naturally understand that we are normally called to a condition of sacrifice. But isn't that, by its very nature, a call to lay down your arms? You see, the unique nature of Peter's proclamation isn't that we are called to have the mind of Christ, but that the mind of Christ is itself a type of tactical defense.

We commonly think of sacrifice being a Christian virtue, but how many times do we stop to see it as a suit of armor? Sacrifice is normally seen as yielding; it is seldom seen as resisting. And yet this is exactly the truth that Peter teaches.

There is no power so powerful to resist daily danger like the sacrificial strength of love. Peter had seen this demonstrated and even experienced it personally in his own life. Whenever he began to go under, it was because of what was deep down in his own heart. He raced out to greet a storm one morning that had terrified him in the night. What was the difference? Was it a difference in degree or intensity? No, the difference was found in the direction of his affection and attention. When he turned from Jesus and looked at the wind and the waves, or even himself, he began to sink. But when he clung to his "life jacket," the Lord Jesus, and was willing to sacrifice himself because of this great love, he had no trouble with the terrible storm.

A word of caution for those who would rush out to sacrifice themselves—this armor cannot be put on through grief. It can only be put on through joy. To be sure, there is a sacrifice that comes from great grief, but it is no armor. Many have sought to abandon this world because of disappointment, but the world followed them to their place of abandonment. The armor of sacrifice, then, must come from gladness, the greatest joy of the human heart—love. Thus, this armor is a breastplate of love.

Seeking to save yourself will not do so. Trying to protect yourself from sickness may be successful for a while, but it will not ultimately be so. You may dodge the dreaded public opinion for a day but not for a lifetime. These weapons eventually wear out. If you want to have a way to guard against temptation, then set your thoughts higher; lift your soul upward. Think of it in the secret place; speak of it in the silence. Dream of it during the night, but most of all live it out where you live. Then realize who it is—it is Christ in you.

Nothing in this life can crucify the desires of the flesh like the joy of the spirit.

> Jesus, help me to live a life of sacrifice. Help me to realize that the only way to save my life is to lose it. Give me the strength to fight off the cares and concerns of this world, the daily desires that would draw me away, through the strength and example of Your sacrificial love. Amen.

Thoughts

34

Angelic Education

To them it was revealed that, not to themselves, but to us they were ministering the things which now have been reported to you through those who have preached the gospel to you by the Holy Spirit sent from heaven; things which angels desire to look into. 1 Peter 1:12

"Things which angels desire to look into." What is it that the angels study? Have you ever asked yourself that question? What subjects do they desire to look into? I would think that they would set their minds on things above, on heavenly things. Wouldn't you? Surely the things that angels think about would surpass the things that we have to think about in our daily, earthly, human lives.

However, when I read what Peter has written, I find that the things that angels think about, study, look into are the things that I ought to be thinking about in my everyday Christian life here on Earth.

So what subjects do the angels study? We're told in the preceding verse. They study "the sufferings of Christ," and they look into "the glories that would follow." In other words, more than anything else, the angels desire to study that path where sacrificial ministry led to spiritual joy. Does that seem strange to you? Does that seem like a subject that is beneath these heavenly beings? If so, then you have surely forgotten what angels really are. The writer of Hebrews says of angels that they are "ministering spirits sent forth to minister for those who will inherit salvation..." Peter knew that.

So, since they are ministering spirits, why wouldn't they study ministry? And if they are going to study ministry, then why wouldn't they study the ministry of the One who became the servant of all? It makes perfect sense, doesn't it? In our lives, we most often study the things that are most closely associated with our nature. The poet naturally studies poetry. The artist spends her time studying the elements of art. A businessman gives himself to fully understanding the intricacies and subtleties of business. So if the angel was created to be a minister, then it follows that he would wish to study the greatest of all ministers.

That's why it's so easy for me to imagine those angels leaning over the balcony of Heaven and gazing on the straight gate and the narrow way that led the Son of Man all the way to Golgotha. You say, "But there was sorrow there." That's right. "But there can't be any sorrow in Heaven." That's right, as well, but don't forget that the very thing that caused sorrow on Earth has been turned into joy in Heaven.

You see, the reason why the selfish heart can't find any fulfillment or joy in studying ministry is because it is just that—a selfish heart. But let a transformation take place. Let that heart be changed from a selfish heart to a servant's heart. Let it be illumined with the light of love. Let it be lifted up into those heavenly heights, and it is that very study which will become its glory.

Do you want to be prepared to think on the theme that the angels ponder? Then answer for yourself this question: "If this very night I were to be in Heaven, would I be filled with joy?" Do you have a heart that is filled with such love and concern for others that you would be delighted to spend eternity studying how to care for them? Or does the thought of giving so much time to the problems and concerns of others seem a sort of cruel and unusual punishment to you? If you do not care for the condition of others, then Heaven won't really be Heaven for you. There would be nothing but pain for you in that place of perpetual ministry.

Heaven isn't to be a home for the selfish. There's no way that such a heart could ever call it home. So if you want to feel at home in Heaven, then make your course of study that which the angels look into. Study the cares and concerns of those around you. Study how to meet the needs of their heart and life. Study the One who became the servant of all. But most of all, look into the greatest, highest, most selfless lesson of real ministry ever taught—the glory of the cross.

Thoughts

35

The Spirit's Chiseling of Our Stony Souls

And the temple, when it was being built, was built with stone finished at the quarry, so that no hammer or chisel or any iron tool was heard in the temple while it was being built. 1 Kings 6:7

As we study these words, it would be easy to deduce that there is no room in the spiritual life for struggles—or even in the conversion to that life. It appears as if the entire edifice rises softly, silently, almost magically. So we are tempted to think that there couldn't be any understanding in that temple for the inner struggles of the soul. But then, on closer inspection, we find that actually the stone's struggle was over before the building ever began. In fact, this verse plainly says that the structure was built with stones that were finished at the quarry. In other words, the materials used in this building were finished before they were ever brought forth and put in place.

What an amazing and encouraging truth those seven little words contain. Before those stones were brought together, they were isolated, separated from each other. Before they were placed into the silent stage of the structure, every single stone had to go through a time of great noise and conflict, a time of being hammered and hewn, chiseled and polished so that they would be in perfect symmetry with each other.

What an obvious hint at the great spiritual conflict that takes place in making us ready to be used by God. Oh, it may be just a flash that passes through our mind, but what a flash it is! It is a flash that lights up our entire experience and shows our very self to us. It says that the silence isn't the first thing, but rather the last thing, that there is a process behind the proportioning before the stone is put in place. It tells us that Saul had his own struggle before Heaven's light flashed before Him, making it so very hard to kick against the goads. It tells me that Nicodemus had to have his solitary stroll that night before he could take up the crucified Christ from the cross' shadow—a walk where he felt deserted by the old yet not quite convinced of the new.

The amazing comfort of this verse is the message that it has for so many struggling souls. Are there times when that inner unrest bothers you? Are there times when you feel tossed on a sea of uncertainty? Are there days when you trod through a desert of doubt? Don't fall into the trap of thinking that this means that there's no place for you in His temple. In fact, this just goes to show that there is a place for you. The struggle you are going through means that you are being made ready for your place there. The cacophony in your conscience is the sound of your stony soul being brought into symmetry—symmetry that will make you a perfect fit for your place in Christ's building. The solitude you feel in your soul doesn't mean that you've been neglected. The struggle in your spirit isn't evidence of the absence of God from your life. In fact, just the opposite—it is the very evidence of His presence. You have been taken into the desert so that you could be made ready. The discomfort you experience is the proof of His interest and affection for you. It is simply the sign that He is preparing you for your special place in His temple. Your desert is the vestibule to Heaven. Bless the Lord, O my soul, and praise His holy name!

Thoughts

36

Asking in the Name of Jesus

Until now you have asked nothing in My name. Ask, and you will receive… John 16:24.

Jesus is seeking the development of His disciples, and the place that He looks to perceive it is in the progress of their prayers. The amazing thing, at least from our human point of view, is where in the prayer He looks. Jesus doesn't look at their invocation but at their motivation. He doesn't look to see what they ask for, but rather why they ask for it, and He measures their prayers accordingly.

When Jesus declares, "Until now you have asked nothing in my name," He means, "You haven't asked in My interest." The problem wasn't that Adam had asked for an apple or that John had asked to sit at His right hand in the Kingdom. The problem was that they both asked for things for themselves.

They weren't looking to fulfill the joy of Jesus but to fulfill their own personal, and even selfish, desires.

It's not that Adam went searching for an apple but that in his search he went looking in the wrong garden. You can get an apple from either Eden or Gethsemane, but in Eden you seek for yourself, while in Gethsemane you seek for another. The first is asking in your name; the second is asking in Jesus' name.

We must purify our desires because it is by those desires that the Master measures our progress as His disciples. It is not so much that we must change what we're asking for, but the purpose behind our prayers.

"And do you seek great things for yourself? Do not seek them…" (Jeremiah 45:5).

I have been asked many times, "Pastor, is it wrong for me to ask God to bless my finances?" The answer to that question is to be found in your reason for asking it. If you want God to bless you so that you can have a bigger, nicer house; a more luxurious automobile; the ability to travel the world in recreation and relaxation—the answer is "yes, you are wrong to ask that of God." However, if you ask the Lord to bless you with financial blessings and your intent is not to get but to give—to share instead of spend, stack up, or save—then I believe that you are not only right in your request, but, dare I say it, righteous.

One day the Devil tempted Jesus—"command that these stones become bread" (Matthew 4:3). It was a temptation because it was said in an attempt to get Jesus to satisfy a personal, physical need. To have done so would have been selfish and therefore sinful. For Jesus to have turned those stones into bread to feed a hungry multitude, or even a widow and her son, would not have been sinful—it would have been sacrificial.

> *"Lord, so many times I have come before You with the desires of my own desert. I have come seeking bread for myself. May the next time I hear the hungry cries of the multitude—or even the one—may I then come asking in Your Name."*

Thoughts

37

Life in a Look

Look to Me, and be saved, All you ends of the earth! For I am God, and there is no other. Isaiah 45:22

What a glorious gaze! The Lord says to all of the earth, "Look to Me, and be saved." This verse tells me that there is life in a look when we look to "the Life." He tells me that I am to look upon Him until I am impressed with His image. I am to look upon Him until His will becomes mine. I am to look upon Him until my weakness is overcome by His strength and He does with me as He pleases for His purposes. I am to look upon Him until His thoughts become my thoughts and His ways become mine. All of this is difficult—impossible, even—before looking to Him, but easy once I have gazed on His glory.

You see, once I look upon Him I no longer have power over myself. His divine life goes through me like a mighty rushing wind. I am made a new creation in Him. I will beat with a new heart, desire with a new will, see with a new eye, and speak with a new tongue. I will be like Him when I have looked to Him, as Isaiah says.

When I look to Jesus, I am transfigured into His image and from glory to glory. He satisfies my desires and longings and will become the desire and object of my heart. He eclipses the moon and sun, extinguishes the stars, just by the power of His person.

I am told that some focus on another object in order to take their mind off of their pain, but here I'm told that gazing on God can remove even the sting of death itself. So, then, let my eyes be fixed on Him, and the ancient wounds from the serpent will be remembered no more. My pain will cease because I will cease to be mine. My life will only be found in Him.

This is life in a look. But don't misunderstand. This is no mere, normal, natural gaze, for no natural man can look upon Him and live. So let your old heart gaze upon Him and die! Let your heart fade and fall to the ground before His great glory, and in its place a new heart will rise up that finds life only in Him.

Thoughts

38

Walking with God

So all the days of Enoch were three hundred and sixty-five years. And Enoch walked with God; and he was not, for God took him.
Genesis 5:23–24

It's said that great men have short biographies. That's certainly true about a man named Enoch. His was the greatest life ever lived in that old world—the world before the flood. He stood head and shoulders above any other antediluvian, yet his life was the shortest of all. His years number less than those of his ancestors. Less is said about his life than anyone else around him. Why is that? Because he lived a life that was far greater than theirs. He lived a life that was more inward and thus was more naturally hidden. The part that burned hotter and brighter in his life was that part that is most often overlooked in the lives of men—his heart, his soul, his spirit.

Enoch's was a life that was hidden in God because the essence of his life was that of His God—love. His was a life that was divine in its walk and, thus, it was seen as insignificant to those of his day—something to be forgotten. Yet there is nothing else that is remembered in that old world. The wars and rumors of wars. Who married or was given in marriage. The business deals, political alliances, and grand parties of that age have all been numbered with the dead—but not Enoch, for by his walk with God he lives forevermore.

What I learn from the short, yet strong life of this man named Enoch is that my walk with God is the evidence of my immortality. What makes man different, unique, from the animals? It is his ability to walk with God. That is something that no other creature in all of His creation can share. I can be lifted above all that is seen and is passing away and enter into that which is unseen and eternal. No low theory of the human mind can take this hope from me. In fact, it's really not even hope, or faith, or something that needs to be proven. It is sight. A present fact. A personal experience of a life that has already begun. My hope of glory is Christ in me. I am immortal before I die. I am already in the promised land of God—seated with Christ in the heavenlies. When death comes looking for me, he will discover that I have already escaped and will have to write the record of his own dismay, "He was not found, for God took him."

Thoughts

39

The Place of Worship

People shall worship Him, Each one from his place... Zephaniah 2:11

The prophet says that there is coming a time when there will no longer be a distinction drawn between the secular and the sacred. This was a startling statement, for this certainly was not the case in His day. During the Jewish dispensation, it was forbidden for men to worship God "each one from his place"—from the spot on which he was standing. In fact, there was only one place where everyone was commanded to worship—Jerusalem. This was the place where the tribes were told to go up. It was from within her gates that the smoke of the incense was to rise. But Zephaniah says that there is a new day dawning, one in which every man will have within his own gates a temple to worship God. There is coming a day, Zephaniah explains, when there will be no need of things or beasts that will carry us from things that are temporal to things that are eternal. It will be done simply by the breath of the Spirit—by a simple movement of the heart.

"In that day," Zechariah declares, "I won't need to leave where I am to go where I must. I will worship from my place—no matter where 'my place' may be. It will become my temple." In that day, every service to man will be considered a service to God. No longer will it be said, "Go up to the House of the Lord," because we will worship from our place. The mother will worship from her place—her altar of sacrifice will be the nursery. The daughter will worship from her place—her offering to God will be her obedience and devotion to her family. The common laborer will worship from his or her place—the simple, menial tasks being viewed as sacrificial service to God. The businessman will worship from his place—his profits will be a gathering for his God. Every song will be a sacred song—all music will have a miraculous melody. Every gift will be garland for Him. My praises will reverberate with His name. My hand will serve in His sanctuary. My feet will follow in His steps. My special grace will minister to His superlative glory. I won't need to stand beside the cross, for I will bear in my own body the dying of the Lord Jesus.

The tremendous thing about this prophetic statement given so long ago by Zephaniah is that the day he saw coming is today! We no longer have to go to Jerusalem, or some other "holy place," to worship God. We can worship; we can serve Him from wherever we are.

To be sure, there are not normally as many witnesses of our worship in our private places. But neither were there many witnesses when Abraham climbed Mount Moriah to offer everything that he had in obedience to the command of his God. No doubt, Mount Moriah was a lonely as any hospital room. It was a solitary battle with the thoughts of his own mind and the desires of his own will. No doubt, he thought that he was being passed over, forgotten, when in actuality he was making history. He was laying the foundation stone for the coming Kingdom of God.

The same is true for you. God's place for you has been Mount Moriah. It has been a place of solitary sacrifice. He may have called you, just like He did Abraham, to climb the mountain "early in the morning." He may have come over you while you were still in the spring of life. Will you then say, "What's the purpose behind all of this? This is nothing but a waste." Is God's shadow a "waste"? When the Spirit hovers over the face of the waters and blocks out the sun, is that a waste? What I am hid in the secret of God's holy place, is that a waste? Is not one hour in God's private classroom worth a whole day in His public school? How glorious His eclipse. How marvelous His hiding. How splendid His obscurity. His shadow proclaims His light, and we dare not ask Earth's broken ones to find a better place than in Him.

Thoughts

40

Thirsty for God

Blessed are those who hunger and thirst for righteousness, For they shall be filled. Matthew 5:6

What an amazing expression of God's grace. The One who is completely holy and totally pure will accept those who even thirst after His righteousness. He doesn't wait until I am made pure to receive me but actually blesses my effort of holiness. He will accept my simple desire of Him, my heart's wish to be like Him, and the longing of my being to be near Him. Though I have yet to reach Him, if I will just look to Him and long to be like Him, He says that He will count it as righteousness for me. Even though I do not claim to be like Him and hesitate to even reach out to touch the hem of His garment, if I will admire His beauty and holiness from afar, He will bless my holy hunger and divine thirst.

However, this verse doesn't teach that you can have salvation apart from God or His goodness. You wouldn't even hunger or thirst for Him if His life were not already working in your life. You wouldn't see in Him any beauty to long for if there were not some spark of His beauty in you. The Beloved Disciple tells us that "we will be like Him, for we will see Him as He is." Thus, your vision of Him is the proof of your likeness to Him. If you were not like Him, you couldn't see Him as He truly is. If His light were not within you, there would be desire in your heart to imitate Him—you wouldn't even fret over not imitating Him.

A man cannot admire that which is outside of his nature. He doesn't seek something that is not like him. That is why my soul's hunger pleads for me and my thirst intercedes on my behalf. The very fact that there is a desire in my heart for holiness shows that His Spirit is even now at the door.

You can cry out for food before you ever even taste it, but you do not have the innate ability to cry out for righteousness until you have first tasted and seen that the Lord, He is good. He has already begun to be beautiful, who has seen the King in His beauty; and he is already starting to be filled, who knows hunger and thirsts after His righteousness.

Thoughts

Honoring the Lord and Encouraging the Saints

He [Jesus] died for us so that, whether we are awake or asleep, we may live together with him. Therefore encourage one another and build each other up, just as in fact you are doing.
—1 Thessalonians 5:10-11

This book, *40 Days of Refreshment*, was originally intended to have forty devotionals. But considering how lavishly the Lord has blessed each of us, it seemed only fitting to add a few more to honor our Lord and to encourage His saints. May God richly bless each of you.

—Pastor Brad Whitt

41

Waiting for Hope

For we through the Spirit eagerly wait for the hope of righteousness by faith. Galatians 5:5

There are days in my life when I look around, and everything seems dark and dreadful. As a matter of fact, there are even days in which is it so dark that I actually have to hope that hope will show up. Now, it's bad enough to wait *with* hope, because having to wait for fulfillment carries its own pain. But to have to wait on hope to even show up, to look out and not see a sliver of hope and yet hold out hope that hope will eventually arrive—that is the greatest kind of patience in the universe. It's Job in the storm; Abraham on the road to Moriah; Moses in the desert of Midian; and Jesus in the Garden of Gethsemane. There is no patience that is harder than the patience that requires that we "endure as seeing Him who is invisible" (Hebrews 11:27). It is waiting for hope to show up.

I can wait through the darkness for the moment when I begin to get a glimpse of the dawn, but when the dawn is invisible to me, that's when I need a supernatural faith. When I begin to see the first blooms of hope, I can say, "Well, summer is on its way." But when the blooms of hope have faded from view, it takes a divine strength to say, "It will bloom again tomorrow." It is divine strength because it is strength that can only be given by the Spirit. Thus, He has given the world a new kind of superhero—those who can wait.

In the past, the superheroes were those who were unwilling, unable to wait. They rushed ever onward, forward, to accomplish what the moment demanded. But He has created a new form of greatness, a fresh form of manliness, because it is in Him, the Son of Man, where that which was a valley yesterday is a mountain today. Waiting has become wonderful. Patience has become powerful. He has shown us that it is possible to look into the cup of sorrow even when there is no star in the sky. He has shown that we can accept the Father's will simply because it is His will. He has shown us that it is possible for our soul to see the cup of sorrow and still not let it go because we know that the Father can see farther than we can.

This is my growing, albeit trembling, desire—to have this divine ability to wait. It's the power that I see Jesus demonstrating in the Garden. To look for a star when there are no stars. Who, when the joy that was set before Him was gone, was still able to stand victorious and say, "I may not be able to see the star, but before my Father it is shining still."

> "Lord, help me to have the power to wait. To hope when hope hasn't shown up, because when I am able to wait for hope, I will have reached the summit of my spiritual strength in You."

Thoughts

_____

_____

_____

_____

_____

42

The Might of Meekness

Blessed are the meek, For they shall inherit the earth. Matthew 5:5

There is a meekness that will not inherit anything. There are two types of calmness that can be found in this world. There is the calmness that is found in a stale, stagnant pond and that which is found in the depths of the mighty sea. One is quiet because it doesn't have anything to say. The other is so because it keeps itself from speaking. That is the greatness and glory of the latter. It is a meekness that remains silent, not because it is empty, but because its depths are full.

Why is it that I love and admire the gentleness of Jesus so? There are countless thousands of silent souls in the world who do not strive or struggle or strain, but I do not call or consider them to be divine. So why has the gentleness of Jesus made Him so great and glorious to me? It is because in Him I find the stillness and quiet calm of His creation. It is a quietness that doesn't exist because it has to or needs to, but because it chooses to do so.

I know that His beautiful sky could begin to frown and thunder and crack and send lightning down on this earth if He so chose, but I am thankful for the gift of a quiet, calm, beautiful day. Yet even in the midst of a cloudless sky, I understand that beneath the sky's silent surface there are depths of countless unspeakable voices, feelings that are unfathomable and powers that are beyond measure. I know by instinct that no man takes His life from Him, but that He and He alone has the power to lay it down—and take it up again. I know that if He so chose, He could call ten thousand angels to make Gethsemane into Sinai. He could change the calm into a tremendous storm, and I respect and revere such strength that will not do what it could do so easily and immediately.

I bow before the might of the Lord's meekness. I stand in absolute amazement in the presence of the One who is so mighty that He could empty Himself of His might. He is more wonderful while hanging on the cross than even when wearing His crown, for He is greater because of what He laid aside than what He possessed. His glory is His shame. His majesty is the surrender of Himself. His royalty is found in His service. His power to rule comes from His power to bear. He is the head over the whole body of humanity; for that reason, He took all the pains of all its members and opened not His mouth. His gentleness has made Him great, and His meekness has inherited the earth.

Thoughts

_____

_____

_____

_____

_____

_____

_____

43

The Law of Liberty

So speak and so do as those who will be judged by the law of liberty.
James 2:12

There are two primary views regarding the human will in the world today. The first says that man is a slave. He is in bondage, shackled hand and foot, to the law. The second says that man is the master of his own actions, he is free, and the law has no dominion over him. Here in our verse, however, James tells us that there is a place of meeting for these two opposing views. He says the reason for this is both assume something that is wrong. James says that both views see "freedom" as the opposite of being "bound." That's why he declares there is something called "the law of liberty," a force whose essence is found in the power of the human will.

So, then, what is this unusual union of two things that seem so contrary to each other? It can be summed up in one simple word—love. Love is the only thing that is both free and bound at the same time. In fact, we often say of people in love that they are "captivated." In other words, they are made a prisoner by their love. Yet they are a prisoner by their own choosing, and they wouldn't see that chain fall for anything in the world. To the one in love, it is a golden chain. It is not a badge of his bondage, but rather of his endless boundaries. It represents the freest thing in his life: the desire of his heart.

My love is the hunger, the prayer, the desire of my heart. It is the most powerful possible exercise of my will. Nothing shows the strength of my will like my love. You see, my love is the strength of myself to go beyond my personal wishes or desires and take another's as my own—to say, "I am yours and you are mine."

James is correct, then, when he says that true love is the coming together of two complete opposites—liberty and law. Love is the most self-sacrificing, and the most self-asserting, of all things—all at the same time. It places its neck in the yoke. It becomes the servant of its object. It takes on another's burden and carries the care of another. But when my heart walks into that prison, it becomes free for the first time. It closes the cuffs yet begins to fly. It takes on heavy weights and then takes wing. It yields to burdensome ties, but those ties become its treasure.

Love's bonds are the beginning of its boundlessness. Every newly fashioned chain is a chariot. I flower by the forgetting of myself. I grow up by growing most underground. I come to the full bloom of summer when I have buried myself.

You see, the human heart can never know true freedom until it has first been mastered. It must be captured before it can even take flight. When my heart has no master, it possesses no power or passion. It doesn't desire to climb the mountain or soar to Heaven. It doesn't rise ready to meet the morning. It only lies in a solemn state of lethargy and death. But when love comes, then my heart finds freedom.

When the Lord became the master of my heart, it was then that I discovered the law of liberty. It was when I was captivated by His beauty, inspired by the touch of His presence, set aflame by the sense of His glory, that I discovered the meaning of freedom. You see, there is no force so strong as that of a subjugated heart, for His law of love is perfect liberty. That's why I say gladly, openly, freely, "Be my heart's ruler, Lord!"

Thoughts

44

Hindsight Is Heavenly

Then Jacob awoke from his sleep and said, "Surely the LORD is in this place, and I did not know it." And he was afraid and said, "How awesome is this place! This is none other than the house of God, and this is the gate of heaven!" Genesis 28:16–17

In a very real sense, the hours of our lives only become reality in retrospect; they become present only when they have already past. We never really understand how meaningful an event is until it has already happened. It is only when creation is complete that we can look at it and say that it has all been very good.

Jacob had been going through a time of great suffering. He was on the run and far away from home. He had no house, no friends, no rest or strength. Night was falling on his life, and the only thing he had was a stone for a pillow. He felt completely forsaken by God. It was as if the Lord had taken flight from his life and left him all alone in the wilderness. He said to himself that the Lord didn't care for, didn't watch over him, and so he laid down and slept a very sorrowful sleep.

He woke, however, to discover that he had been completely wrong in his assessment of his situation. Instead of being far from God, he found that he'd never been more near to Him. In the hour that

He thought he was all alone, he discovered that angels had been watching over him and the presence of the Lord was all around him. He had unknowingly become the recipient of a tremendous blessing, and now he longed for nothing more than to return to that time that he had loathed. The Lord had been in that place, and he hadn't even realized it.

How many times has this been true in your life? How often have you thought, in the midst of your sorrow, that the Lord had left you all alone? How many times have you slept in sorrow and wished to never wake up? But when you woke, you found that the darkness you dreaded was nothing more than a delusion. The Lord had been right there with you all along.

Your aspirations must not only be for the future but for the glory of those things that have already passed. You must realize that even your yesterdays were very good. You must discover the glory that is inherent in the path that the Lord has led you and be able to say of the tears you've shed and toil you've endured that this was Heaven's gate!

Thoughts

45

The Power in Being Poor

Blessed are the poor in spirit, For theirs is the kingdom of heaven.
Matthew 5:3

To be "poor in spirit" seems a really strange goal for me to seek to attain. However, while it might at first appear to be easy and unheroic, it is actually one of the most difficult and heroic things in the world. You see, while it may be easy to be poor spiritually, that is really not the same thing as being poor in spirit.

Only those who are truly rich spiritually can be poor in spirit, for to be poor in spirit means that I am aware of the fact that I am nothing and have nothing. Before I can have that conscious awareness, I must have begun to be something. Isn't it only as I begin to know my true state that my ignorance starts to be revealed to me? Isn't the fact of my own sinfulness made apparent as I look on the One who is infinitely pure and holy?

A heart that is dead is totally unaware of its deadness. That's why it is only in that moment when I fall under the weight of my own spiritual sickness that I first learn of my overwhelming weakness. The closer I draw to Christ, the more I realize just how far off I follow Him. My humility rises with my revelation.

When I was a young child, I wanted to reach up and grab the sun, but it was when I learned the laws of creation that I became poor in spirit. My knowledge of God works in much the same way. As long as I am apart from Him, away from Him, I am satisfied with myself. The reason for this is because I don't have a standard by which to measure my fallen estate. However, when I draw near to Jesus, then I see myself as I truly am.

It is in the light of His holiness that I see my darkness. It is in His majesty that I measure my meanness. It is by His incorruption that I become conscious of my corruption. It is in the presence of His wealth that I come to grips with my poverty. In fact, my confession of sin is really the result of His holiness. It's the dawning of His glorious light that reveals my utter darkness.

So don't say that being poor in spirit is something that is easy or unheroic. It is actually proof that Heaven's kingdom has come—"for theirs *is* the kingdom of heaven." Don't despair over the revelation of your nothingness, for this just proves that you have beheld a higher standard of measurement—the perfect measure of the stature of Jesus Christ. Gaze more and more on Jesus, for it is in the brightness of His beauty that you will begin to loathe your own impurity. Then, in the blaze of glory that no human eye has seen, you will fall at His feet and be lifted up—a new man in Him!

Thoughts

_____

_____

_____

_____

_____

_____

46

Consecrating Common Things

Then the manna ceased on the day after they had eaten the produce of the land; and the children of Israel no longer had manna, but they ate the food of the land of Canaan that year. Joshua 5:12

Joshua tells us that the miraculous manna suddenly ceased. That food, which had come down from above since the days of the nation's infancy, would now come up from the ground since that they had matured into manhood. The powerful Presence that had been their guide while they wandered in the wilderness would now give to them the power to guide themselves. Until now every man had been fed by the hand of God, but from this time forward every man was to feed one another. The manna would no longer miraculously and spontaneously fall from the skies. Now it would be the husband's responsibility to feed his wife, the parent's responsibility to feed their children, and the strong's responsibility to feed the weak. For forty years, they had been nourished by way of the heavenly food, but from this point forward they would eat of the food of Canaan. In the absence of the miraculous manna, they would gather from the food of the land.

Would such a drastic change cause you to worry or fret? Would hearing this make you want to go back to the wilderness and once again taste Heaven's manna? Would you miss the miraculous, unexplainable manna every morning? Would it bother to have to go back to the "old way" of gathering grain because it is part of the first laws of creation? Do you think that God's greatest gifts are those things that come riding in invisible chariots? Do you think that God's love is less spectacular when you are able to watch it work? Do you think that God's care is less amazing when it happens the same way every day?

If so, you have missed the higher meaning and greater glory of this amazing account. It was not the manna that was most amazing. It was the simple, common, everyday food of the land. When we eat of the food of the land, we may not be nourished by angelic messengers like Elijah, but that doesn't make our "messengers" any less "heavenly." You see, the very same God who sent the manna also set the seasons. He's the One who sends the sun and the rain, as well as the love of human hearts and service of human hands. He doesn't feed your neighbors with angel's food so that you can have the opportunity of being a blessing by giving them of your food. He doesn't send the ravens into the deserts of your life because He doesn't want to rob your neighbor of the blessing of coming and giving to you. Don't fuss and fret over the fact that the manna has stopped, but rather rejoice that because of God's great love you are able to eat of, and share in, the produce of the land.

Thoughts

_____

_____

_____

_____

_____

47

The Power of Personal Ministry

Now it came to pass on the next day that Moses went into the tabernacle of witness, and behold, the rod of Aaron, of the house of Levi, had sprouted and put forth buds, had produced blossoms and yielded ripe almonds. Numbers 17:8

Have you ever stopped to consider why it was only the rod of Aaron, the emblem of the priesthood and picture of sacrificial love, that budded? So many times, we dream of and desire the power and glory of the world's kingdoms. We look with longing at the king's scepter—the symbol of personal might. However, have you ever pondered why, out of the twelve, it wasn't the scepter of the king but the staff of the priest that budded?

This is a very powerful picture indeed. That which is able to bring forth blossoms and fruit is more than a mere ruler; it is a creator that inspires even more life. That's why I believe the priest's staff was mightier than the king's scepter—because even though a king's rod can subdue life, only Aaron's rod could create it.

Have you ever invested in the power of sacrifice to see new buds, flowers, and fruits brought into this world? There are seeds of life deep down in the valley that have not bloomed because sunlight has yet to reach them. They are living in the darkness and shadow, waiting for the warmth and life of light. If there were only some way that light could reach them and warm them, they would surely burst forth with flowers; the desert would burst into praise, and the wilderness would be glad.

You, Child of God, have the light and warmth of your Father. Will you go? Will you bear His light to those who are in such desperate need? Will you descend into the dark valley where lonely limbs cannot bring forth their buds because of a lack of the sun? Will you carry to the dark and desolate spots of this world His radiant light?

The rod of rule would surely crush the seeds of life because of their lack of beauty, but the staff of sacrifice can bring them into full blossom. It can wake them with the buds of hope; it can touch them with the tears of human sympathy; it can encourage them with the warmth of another. Such is the power of personal ministry.

If your brother has fallen into sin or despair, do not speak to him from the height of your mountain. Go down to him and meet with him where he is. Go down and tell him that you are with him. Tell him that his fall has not made you his superior. Go down and restore, yes, but restore such a one with a spirit of meekness. Don't do so from the height but from the level of a conscious awareness of a common weakness. Then the buds will burst forth in the sunshine of your sacrifice. The blossoms will unfold in your light. Your rod will become as Aaron's rod and your kingdom the throne of the Lamb.

Thoughts

48

The Rest Jesus Gives

Come to Me, all you who labor and are heavy laden, and I will give you rest. Matthew 11:28

In this verse, Jesus issues a call to the entirety of humanity because we all "labor" or are "heavy laden." Some suffer under the weight of toil while others weep from the incapacitating burden that toil so often brings. However, whether it is active or passive, every one of us experiences suffering. So Christ speaks to us through the one thing that every single one of us has in common—the cross.

What does Jesus promise? Does He say, "Come to me, all those of you who are working, and you will never have to work again; come to me, those of you who are bearing under tremendous burden, and you will never be burdened again?" No; He says, "Come…and I will give you REST. Come, all of you who trod this world's road, and I will give you the power to trod more abundantly. Come, all of you are carrying the weight of a heavy cross, and I will give you the strength to carry it more lightly. Come, all of you who are working, and I will give you the ability to work even more. Come, all of you who are burdened down, and I will give you the power to press on."

The promise of power that the Lord offers is the reality of rest that comes from within. Jesus says to us, "You will find rest for your souls." If there were only a way for us to find rest for our souls, then surely we would have the ability to rest anywhere. Those who cry out in the dark hours of the night for some thorn to be removed perhaps have never considered that there is something else that is sufficient for their suffering—a rest that comes from within. What a blessing it would be if, even while the thorn remained, you could be made to forget its pain! What if you could be so caught up in a great and glorious thought that you became oblivious to not only its pain but its very presence? What if that which causes you to crumble under its great burden were to be counterbalanced by the greater weight of eternal glory?

This is the promise of Jesus for you. The rest that you long for must come from within, not from without. The things of this world will never bring this rest, and the loss of those things cannot take it from you. If you will simply seek to draw close to Christ's heart and feel His great love for you, then you will be independent of the green pastures and still waters—and then ALL of your pastures will be green, and your waters will be still. Your thorn will be transformed into your flower; your weight will become your wing; your cross will become your crown of glory when you find the rest He has promised—rest for your soul.

Thoughts

www.ingramcontent.com/pod-product-compliance
Lightning Source LLC
Chambersburg PA
CBHW071729090426
42738CB00011B/2421